Classic Civil Aircraft: 3
DE HAVILLAND
COMET

Classic Civil Aircraft: 3

DE HAVILLAND COMET

PHILIP J. BIRTLES

F-BGNX

LONDON

IAN ALLAN LTD

Contents

First published 1990

ISBN 0 7110 1947 9

Published by Ian Allan Ltd, Shepperton, Surrey; and printed by Ian Allan Printing Ltd at their works at Coombelands in Runnymede, England

Front cover:
Comet 4C G-BDIF of Dan-Air taxying to the north satellite pier at Gatwick Airport, May 1979. *Anthony Wirkus*

Back cover, top:
Comet 4C, XS235, is a flying laboratory with the A&AEE Boscombe Down.

Back cover, bottom:
Comet 4B G-APND of BEA Airtours being towed from the parking area to the central pier at Gatwick Airport, July 1972. *Anthony Wirkus*

Note: All drawings originally appeared in the *de Havilland Gazette* and are reproduced by kind permission of British Aerospace

Preface

Philip Birtles has produced a very thorough record of the de Havilland 106, better known as the Comet, from its design stage through its development and flight testing leading on to its entry into passenger service in May, 1952.

The subsequent history is well covered and brings back many happy memories to me.

The grounding of the Comet after the Elba and Naples accidents was a great blow to us all at Hatfield and undoubtedly meant that de Havillands would have to work very hard to re-establish their good reputation in the Aviation World.

The Comet 4 proved to be a very reliable and much liked aeroplane and restored de Havilland's reputation.

It is now 41 years since the Comet 1 made its first flight and set a standard of air travel in speed and smoothness of flight that air travellers throughout the world enjoy today.

Those of us who were privileged to play a part in the development of the Comet can look back with pride and pleasure on the achievements of the team at de Havillands that were responsible for designing and building the Comet, the world's First Jet Transport.

J. Cunningham
June, 1990

Introduction

To people who have had an interest in aviation for 40 years or more, the Comet jet airliner will be fairly familiar, but the younger generation may be unaware of the pioneering spirit of the de Havilland enterprise in developing — largely from its own resources — the world's first commercial jet airliner.

From such modest beginnings, with a pioneering aviation spirit equal to any other major aviation achievement, de Havilland laid the firm foundations for today's jet transport aircraft flying millions of people all over the world, and the fortunate few at twice the speed of sound.

A great deal was learned, unfortunately the hard way, by de Havilland and BOAC, on the behaviour of metal under extreme stress, and although those lessons were well learned and communicated widely, problems with metal fatigue still exist today, particularly in the less well maintained geriatric jets.

The de Havilland Comet is one of the world's significant aerospace milestones and this book attempts to record the progress of the aircraft as it happened, from early triumph to disaster, and then rising again out of the ashes.

I would like to record my thanks to Mr K. J. Meadows of RAE Farnborough, Flt Lt Alan Snowball from the A&AEE Boscombe Down, and a number of long-serving de Havilland employees for the assistance with information and advice in the preparation of this book. Also, special thanks to my wife, Martha, for the major part she has played in the production of the manuscript.

Philip J. Birtles
Stevenage
August 1989

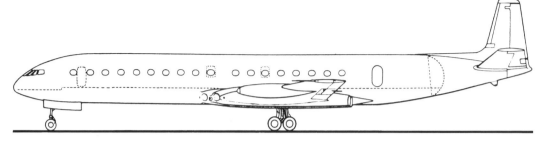

Conception

During World War 2, the British and American governments came to an agreement on the development of aircraft for the war effort to avoid needless duplication of valuable resources. In effect, Britain would concentrate on the design, development and production of combat aircraft, such as fighters and bombers, while the USA would undertake the provision of transport aircraft. This, of course, did not mean that some fine fighters and bombers did not evolve from American companies, prime examples being the Mustang and Thunderbolt long-range fighters and the Flying Fortress and Liberator day bombers which made a massive contribution to the winning of the war by the Allies.

Britain did not use resources on transport aircraft, allowing the USA to build up an impressive lead of reliable, conventional commercial airliners to take advantage of expanding international air routes once peace was declared. The USA, as it does today, had the advantage not only of a strong aircraft industry with lucrative government contracts, but also a large domestic market which could absorb healthy initial production runs of these airliners, making them more cost-effective in the export market.

However, it was not all bad for Britain. In striving for ever better fighter performance, Sir Frank Whittle had against all odds, both political and industrial, developed a practical jet engine which first flew in the specially built Gloster E.28/39 from Cranwell on 15 May 1941. This was only an experimental combination to test the new form of propulsion and allow development of more powerful and reliable power plants.

The development of the jet engine was taken up by a number of the engine manufacturers, in particular Rolls-Royce and the de Havilland Engine Company, the latter under the leadership of Maj Frank Halford. Maj Halford had, in fact, started the design of a jet engine, to be known as the Halford

Below:
Even in its unpainted finish the de Havilland Comet was a simple, yet graceful design. The prototype originally flew in the Class B markings G-5-1.

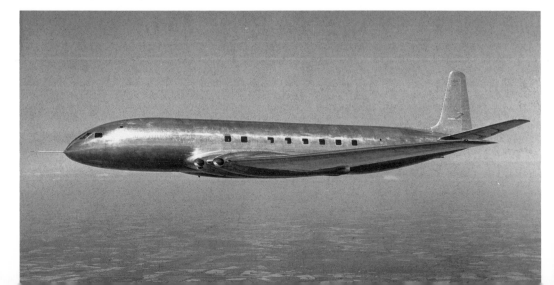

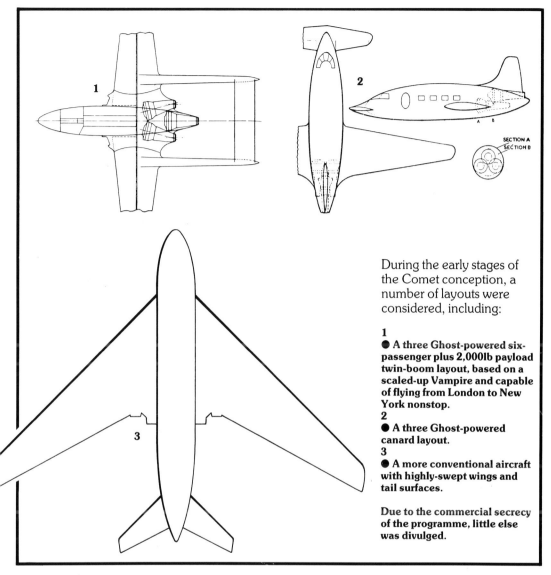

During the early stages of the Comet conception, a number of layouts were considered, including:

1
● **A three Ghost-powered six-passenger plus 2,000lb payload twin-boom layout, based on a scaled-up Vampire and capable of flying from London to New York nonstop.**
2
● **A three Ghost-powered canard layout.**
3
● **A more conventional aircraft with highly-swept wings and tail surfaces.**

Due to the commercial secrecy of the programme, little else was divulged.

H1, in 1941 with a very similar layout to the Whittle design. It had what was known as a centrifugal compressor, which was low risk — but not the most efficient form of layout — the smaller diameter axial flow jet engine later providing much improved performance. Not only was de Havilland advancing technology in the design of the jet engine, but it also pioneered production techniques for these new high speed power plants. The piston-engined aircraft had practically reached its limitations, and for speeds in excess of 500mph the jet engine was the logical method of power, even though early examples developed low thrust, had a modest endurance and poor acceleration.

The Halford H1 engine was codenamed 'Supercharger' and with development was later to become the DH Goblin, the first jet engine to enter full production. So advanced were de Havilland engines that the Gloster Meteor made its maiden flight on 5 March 1943 powered by a pair of H1 engines, due to the non-availability of the selected Rolls-Royce Welland.

Construction of the first Goblin commenced on 8 August 1941 and only 248 days later the engine was first run on the testbed at Hatfield. This was despite having had to overcome major problems in thermo-dynamics, the use of new materials, and detailed design to keep loss of performance to a minimum, the main areas concentrated upon being the compressor and combustion chambers. The engine was cleared to fly two years after the start of design and, following its debut in the all-new

Meteor, a single Goblin powered the de Havilland Vampire which was first flown from Hatfield by Geoffrey de Havilland Jnr on 20 September 1943.

Development of the Goblin engine progressed as lessons were learned and the more powerful de Havilland Ghost engine was produced in two major forms, one with the split air intakes, test flown in a specially adapted high altitude Vampire and later to power the de Havilland Venoms, and the other with a single nose intake to be used in the proposed de Havilland Comet jet airliner. While the Vampire tested the engines at the high speed, high altitude end of the performance envelope, in which John Cunningham gained the absolute altitude record of 59,446ft on 23 March 1948, a pair of Avro Lancastrians had their outer Merlins replaced with Ghost engines for lower altitude endurance testing. The Lancastrian was a very basic transport derivative of the Lancaster bomber, and these adapted aircraft could cruise quite happily on the two Ghost engines, with the Merlins shut down.

Meanwhile, during World War 2, Britain had not totally abandoned all thoughts of postwar commercial airliner development. On an official tour of the US aerospace industry, Sir Ralph Sorley and Sir Roy Fedden were shown some of the work being done on civil airliners. As a result of their report, the British government announced its intention to investigate the development of future civil transport aircraft, leading to the formation of the Brabazon Committee, chaired by Lord Brabazon of Tara, one of the early British aviation pioneers. The object was to recommend a number of aircraft types worthy of development which were not in direct competition with the already established US market, or which could demonstrate a significant advance.

The design targets recommended to British industry in May 1943, included the Type IV which was broadly specified as a jet-propelled transatlantic mail plane, capable of carrying a ton of payload and having the crew housed in a pressure cabin to

Below:
The Comet prototype was eventually painted in BOAC markings and registered G-ALVG.

Right:
Wind tunnel models were made for slow-speed testing of the Comet shape.

allow high altitude cruise. Other aircraft to emerge from the range of specifications was the de Havilland Dove as the Committee's Type 5B to replace the Rapide; the Type I which became the giant but unsuccessful Brabazon airliner; Type IIA which was a DC-3 replacement produced by Airspeed as the Ambassador, powered by a pair of Bristol Centaurus piston engines; the prop-jet, Type IIB category, which resulted in the unsuccessful Armstrong Whitworth Apollo and the highly popular Rolls-Royce Dart-powered Vickers Viscount; and the Type III which was considered by Avro, but did not proceed beyond the preliminary design stages.

In June 1943, official sanction was given to de Havilland to proceed with project design of the Type IV, but any further progress was limited by the country's continuing war effort on combat aircraft. The seeds were sown for a viable and competitive British aircraft industry once peace came again in Europe.

De Havilland had already looked at the possibility of adapting the prewar DH95 Flamingo to jet power, by replacing the original piston engines with a pair of Goblin engines. However, apart from very short flights, the aircraft payload would consist almost entirely of fuel. It was realised as a result of this study that a faster higher-flying aircraft needed

to be developed, and no useful experience could be gained with the Flamingo.

The British government did not wish to fall into the trap of specifying uncommercial aircraft, so while providing encouragement — and eventually financial support — the most effective way to progress was seen to be direct contact between the manufacturers and the emerging interests in the postwar airlines, including the state-owned BOAC as far as commercial jet operations were concerned.

The Brabazon Committee was enlarged on 2 June 1943 to include representation from the manufacturers and potential commercial operators. Up to this time the project design team had looked at a four Goblin-powered, short-range civil design, but there was still no prospect of a practical longer range aircraft without more extensive wind tunnel studies and further research.

During the latter part of 1943, more detailed work was undertaken on an aircraft with a capacity for 20 passengers. It was similar in layout to the twin-boomed Vampire jet fighter with three Goblin engines clustered in the tail of the fuselage nacelle, avoiding power losses due to long jet pipes. The Goblin engine developed just over 3,000lb thrust and gave this aircraft a range of about 700 miles. This was still a long way off transatlantic range, but at least could be carrying a more commercial payload than simply urgent mail.

During the winter months of 1943-44 the aircraft was studied in a number of larger sizes, including power from three of the as yet untried Ghost engines which were expected to develop 5,000lb of thrust each, a considerable improvement over the Goblin. Variations in the general layout were considered, moving from the twin-boom to an

11

Left:
The first Comet fuselage was completed in the Experimental hangar before moving to the centre for wing assembly.

Below left:
A complete fuselage was produced for the Comet structural test programme.

Bottom left:
The wings were assembled to the prototype's fuselage, ready for the Ghost engine installation.

Right:
The prototype was weighed prior to roll-out and the second fuselage was built alongside before assembly to the wings in the main assembly hall.

aft-placed straight wing with canards or foreplanes, to balance the three engines grouped in the rear fuselage. This was probably the earliest application of canards to a jet aircraft, now often considered essential to maintain effective control in today's highly unstable combat aircraft.

Following studies by Dr Roxbee Cox at the Ministry of Aircraft Production, it became apparent that the lack of range problem could be overcome by propeller turbines. However, the propjet was a complex powerplant with the addition of its reduction gearing and all the other ancillaries, besides which, no suitable engines existed. Later, propjets were to be developed for long-range commercial use, but were outclassed by the faster pure jet aircraft when better economy was achieved. The propjet then became the mainstay of the shorter range commuter and feeder markets.

On 19 April 1944, the relative merits of the three Ghost-engined aircraft and a twin propjet aircraft with a 1-ton payload were discussed. The decision was made to commence development immediately on the pure jet transport, to be followed as soon as possible by the propjet aircraft with the longer range. It was also agreed soon after that it was not then practical to draw up a detailed list of requirements for the jet transport, as had been done with the more conventional aircraft, since there were too many unknowns.

De Havilland remained convinced that the pure jet was destined for long-range operations, and one way of achieving this was to make longer runways available for take-off with a higher fuel load. The experience with the early flight trials of the Vampire fighter confirmed the absence of vibration and reduced noise, which would save passenger fatigue on long flights. Jet travel would be a transformation

from the current discomfort experienced with piston-engined airliners.

BOAC supported the jet airliner programme from the earliest stage, particularly in achieving a sufficient range for transatlantic operations, which were a key to the success of the aircraft. Longer runways were becoming available, particularly on either side of the Atlantic and the aircraft were required to fly at the greatest possible height and speed. If 500mph could be achieved for a mail carrier, the rates earned would adequately pay for the more expensive mode of transport.

The three Ghost-engined Vampire layout was favoured in August 1944, and by mid-October it was presented to the Brabazon Committee with accommodation for six passengers and a 2,000lb load of mail. In February 1945 a high-speed wind tunnel model of this layout was delivered to RAE Farnborough for investigation of its practicality.

While design continued on this layout, providing a good research base, it was realised that a more practical and less specialised aircraft was required, which could be effectively achieved using four Ghost engines for power. The overall layout was more traditional, the first estimates being available in March 1945. The studies considered an 8ft 6in diameter fuselage, holding 24 passengers seated three-abreast or a 10ft diameter fuselage seating between 24 and 36 passengers four-abreast.

The problems to be overcome in the development of a practical jet airliner were massive. In fact the programme was on a similar scale of technological challenge to the development of the supersonic Concorde two decades later, but at a fraction of the real cost. With Britain's lead in jet engine development, a practical and economically competitive jet airliner would give the country a

Above:
Once overseas flying started, the Class B markings were replaced by the registration G-ALVG.

chance to gain a major foothold in the postwar airliner market ahead of the USA.

Amongst the challenges for the design team was the need to produce an aircraft which could fly higher and faster than any other airliner, and which would be comfortable for the average passenger who would not require a medical to prove he was superhuman before travelling in this high performance aircraft. The large cabin would have to be pressurised and the air would have to be controlled in both temperature and humidity to maintain a comfortable environment. Aircraft navigation and air traffic control would have to cope with the higher speed of operation, yet the airliner would have to fit into normal traffic patterns with docile handling at lower speeds.

Some research had been started on swept-back wings to delay the onset of compressibility at higher velocities, as the speed of sound was approached. As a result, a study was made of a tailless airliner with a wing sweep-back of 40°, and four Ghost engines mounted under the wings near the trailing edge. The all-up weight would have been 75,000lb.

To test the practicality of this configuration, the DH108 — sometimes unofficially known as the 'Swallow' — was produced to Spec E.18/45, a total of three prototypes being built for low and high speed research, by adapting a Vampire fuselage nacelle to take a thin swept wing. A swept-back fin and rudder were mounted above the jet pipe exhaust and the need for a horizontal tail was eliminated by the use of elevons on the wing trailing edge to give combined pitch and roll control.

The first DH108, TG283, which was almost a half-scale model of the proposed airliner, made its maiden flight from the long runway at Woodbridge on 15 May 1946, in the hands of Geoffrey de Havilland Jnr, the Chief Test Pilot and elder son of the founder. However, by the time this experimental aircraft had flown, it had already been

determined that the elimination of all horizontal surfaces was not entirely practical. The effective elevator movement arm from the centre of gravity was so small that the effectiveness of the flaps was limited. Therefore, for a given wing area and runway length, the take-off and landing weight was less than if a tailplane with normal elevators was used. This was sufficient to make a tailless layout uneconomical.

At the end of May 1946, a complete brochure was presented showing an aircraft with a more conventional layout featuring 40° swept-back wings and horizontal tail surfaces. The all-up weight of 93,000lb allowed a payload of 5,000lb to be carried across the Atlantic. A better formula had to be found to be more economical.

After the DH108 had been flying for about 10 weeks in July 1946, it was determined that the wing sweep-back was uneconomic, both because of the lower maximum lift coefficient and also the higher structural weight of the increased wing length for a given span. The elimination of wing sweep-back improved lift and reduced weight, almost doubling the Atlantic payload to 9,200lb. With the level of knowledge then available, and the lower power of the jet engines, there was no alternative but to go for a more orthodox design with a modest sweepback of 20°, as much as for the centre of gravity as for aerodynamic reasons. It would certainly ease the flight development problems of a totally new concept in air travel, the performance and timetable of which had to be guaranteed at the project stage. The swept-wing research was not lost though, as it provided a great deal of knowledge in swept-wing design, the DH108 became the first

Above:
The main bulk of the flight development programme was shared by the two Comet prototypes. G-ALZK was the second aircraft, later used for BOAC route-proving.

British aircraft to go supersonic on 9 September 1948, flown by John Derry, with power coming from a 3,250lb thrust Goblin engine. A remarkable achievement on such a low cost and modest power.

During the months of August and September 1946, the basic specification of the new jet airliner was worked out with BOAC, culminating in a telephone call by Geoffrey de Havilland Snr to the airline on Friday 27 September, dealing with a final major point to allow detail design to proceed. That same evening, his son, Geoffrey, was killed while test-flying the DH108 in a practice attempt on the world air speed record. Control was lost in a dive over the Thames Estuary, the aircraft pitching violently forward, breaking off the wings. By 7 October it had been determined that the engine was not the cause of the accident, and John Cunningham was appointed Chief Test Pilot of the de Havilland Aircraft Company in Geoffrey's place.

By November 1946, the airliner had been designated the DH106 and a complete weight and performance statement was prepared. At an all-up weight of 100,000lb the aircraft was estimated to be capable of carrying a payload of 7,000lb, equal to 24 passengers, from London to Gander, allowing for a 100mph headwind and with fuel diversion allowances. For the Empire routes an all-up weight of 96,500lb would carry a 10,000lb payload equal to 32 passengers over stage lengths of 2,200 miles. As a comparison with today's Boeing 747 Jumbo jet, the all-up weight can be 836,000lb with a payload of 151,800lb, equal to 336 passengers plus cargo, an improvement in efficiency with modern

technology of some 250%. The statement also included guarantees of payload, range, cruising speed and runway lengths required. It is a great credit to the de Havilland design team that despite many detailed changes during the development programme, the original guarantees were met on cost and on time.

The aircraft flew two years and nine months after detail design started, and it entered service two years and nine months after that. Five-and-a-half years were about right for a conventional airliner produced by the British aircraft industry in the years just after World War 2; considering the world's first jet airliner had many innovative features, the time scale was very creditable.

Although the first two aircraft were in effect prototypes to be used for flight testing, such was the confidence in the advances being made, that production was commenced at the same time of the aircraft for the airlines. This challenging new programme did not represent a larger step forward than was judged correct at the time, to minimise the risk. The major difference from subsequent programmes was that due to low initial production on the basis of an order for only 16 aircraft, the test programme could not be shared by the first half-dozen aircraft off the line. The bulk of the flight testing had to be with the two prototypes, the first production aircraft being used to confirm the results and achieve certification. With modern jet airliner programmes, a much greater investment is made in tooling to spread the test programme over more aircraft, to build up hours more rapidly, ensuring earlier deliveries.

The two development prototypes were ordered on a commercial basis by the Ministry of Supply, not as a 'cost plus development' contract. The price paid was on the basis of up to 50 total orders to achieve a breakeven, a very modest number by today's standards, especially for such an advanced programme. The Ghost engines were already under development for military purposes at a cost of about £2.5 million and only needed adaptation for the single intake for the Comet and civil certification.

In an effective effort to reduce competition, little information was issued by de Havilland. It was widely known that a jet airliner was being studied, but as far as the competition was concerned, the USA in particular, it was a long-term project that might or might not materialise. R. E. Bishop, the Chief Designer, kept a model in his office of a tailless swept-wing airliner project to mislead the many important visitors. Security was tight in the factory where parts were being made for the first aircraft and the large ground test rigs were kept screened off to give no hint of progress or configuration. This high commercial security, equal to national military secrecy, was successfully maintained until the maiden flight. Even when the first aircraft was rolled out of the Experimental Shop on 2 April 1949 for its engine runs, it was shrouded in mist, helping to hide it from prying eyes. But, before the maiden flight, much testing had to be done on the new systems, materials and techniques to be employed in the radical new design.

On 24 July 1947, a modified Avro Lancastrian flying test bed made its maiden flight with a pair of Ghost engines replacing the outboard Merlins. To maintain the tight flight development schedule, a second Lancastrian was also adapted and the two aircraft flew a total of 425hr, equal to 1,700 engine hours, before the Comet itself took over the flying programme. The Lancastrians were able to give practical experience of the air intake shape and ram effect, fuel system operation, engine relight, jet-pipe cooling and many other features within the relatively low speeds and altitude restriction of 25,000ft of the test aircraft. To achieve testing at speeds and altitudes more representative of the Comet, a specially adapted Vampire with extended wingtips, a pressure cabin and powered by a Ghost engine was able to investigate the engine performance up to nearly 60,000ft, higher than the Comet cruising altitude, more than a year before the Comet's maiden flight. On 28 June 1948, the Ghost became the first jet engine to gain civil type approval for public transport after a flight development programme of 11 months.

With the higher anticipated aerodynamic loads on the control surfaces, a need was seen for power assistance, and these were developed on the DH108 from May 1946, three years before the Comet flew, keeping the technical risk to a minimum. This was complemented by a full scale control system rig set up in the factory and operated continuously for over three years, to determine the practical endurance of the component parts, to assess and improve failure rates and provision for spares and overhaul.

Although the nose shape could be tested theoretically in the wind tunnel, it was found desirable to try it out in full scale to check the effect of rain at low approach speeds and also to assess the view in general for the pilots. Fortunately, the fuselage diameter of the Airspeed Horsa troop-carrying glider was the same as the rear frame of the Comet nose, allowing a mock up of the Comet nose to be fitted to a Horsa glider. John Cunningham was towed aloft in this adaptation during the winter of 1946-47 in search of elusive rainstorms.

The traditional structural test programmes were undertaken, but with special, additional work to consider the new higher stresses produced by pressurisation of the fuselage. Details were tested individually, followed by testing of the larger assemblies in the normal way. The first production wing was used in a dynamic fatigue test programme while attached to a representative section of fuselage. Hydraulic rams subjected the wing to up and down stresses, deflecting the wing by up to 3ft at the tips, simulating many thousands of flights, well beyond the anticipated normal aircraft operations. Static loads were applied to the main undercarriage units mounted on this rig, testing both the undercarriage and the surrounding wing structure. These tests included drag and side load effect, drop tests to simulate heavy landings, and 16,000 retraction tests with the bearings lubricated by a mixture of grease and sand to determine wear. The complete nosewheel assembly, including pilots, steering, was mounted on a suitably ballasted three-ton truck chassis, and driven for 120 miles around the airfield at speeds of up to 40mph to check the nosewheel steering.

A decompression chamber was installed at Hatfield to allow testing of major assemblies in the cold rarefied air conditions of high altitudes. The chamber was able to achieve minus 70°C and simulate altitudes up to 70,000ft. The chamber was large enough to accommodate sections of the full-scale Comet fuselage to test the pressurisation and air conditioning equipment. The cabin pressure of the Comet 1 was up to 8.25lb/sq in, putting high loads on the cabin structure.

The fuselage nose was the first section to be tested in the chamber and was subjected to 2,000 applications of 9lb/sq in pressure, during the course of which the leak rate reduced.

Testing of larger sections of the fuselage to greater loads was undertaken, immersed in water tanks, with the specimen also filled with water. Due to water being virtually incompressible, little energy is stored when it is pressurised. Therefore, if there should be a failure in the fuselage specimens, the internal and external pressures immediately equalise, avoiding explosive destruction of the test piece and allowing detailed examination of the damage. If

Above:
The second prototype retained the large single mainwheel undercarriage of the first aircraft, but had suppressed elevator mass balances.

Below:
Canadian Pacific was the first export customer for the Comet, to the improved Srs 1A standard.

air had been used in these tests, the specimen would have been destroyed like a burst balloon. Both the nose section and a representative parallel section of the cabin were tested under water and were periodically subjected to 16.5lb/sq in, double the service pressure, to give an adequate safety margin. The windows and frames were tested exhaustively, including daily pressurisations for three years, one window surviving a load of 100lb/sq in

It was believed that static testing of the aircraft structure with a large margin of safety would adequately determine any likely sources of fatigue cracking that might indicate structural weakness. As future events were to show, this method of testing was not sufficient to avoid disaster. Dynamic testing was also essential.

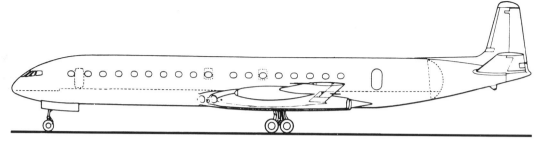

Testing and Early Sales

Despite the embargo on publicity to protect against transatlantic competition, orders were placed during 1946 and 1947 by BOAC for eight aircraft and British South American Airways for six. The latter was merged into BOAC and the contract was confirmed for a total of 14 Comet 1s at a fixed price with performance and delivery dates guaranteed.

In April 1949, de Havilland made an introductory statement, giving some preliminary information about the Comet jet airliner, this statement being published in the *de Havilland Gazette* bi-monthly magazine. In the introduction, the company thanked the press for their restraint in publicising the development of the Comet, not only to forestall competition, but also to maintain a confidence in the programme, which due to the long period of gestation would create an impression of difficulties being experienced, when in fact none existed. It

was confirmed that, including the two prototypes, a total of 16 Comets were being built against firm orders, production of which started directly from the design stage, to minimise service entry delays.

The Comet was designed for worldwide operations providing a fast service on British Commonwealth routes and intercontinental services generally. The higher operating speeds would not only give the Comet an advantage over the competition with shorter and more comfortable journeys, but it would also make the aircraft more productive. Despite its high speed the Comet needed to have good slow-flying capabilities to fit into existing traffic patterns around the busy airports. The wing loading and stalling speed were very similar to existing propeller-driven airliners. It was to be capable of normal operation out of existing major airfields. However, due to its

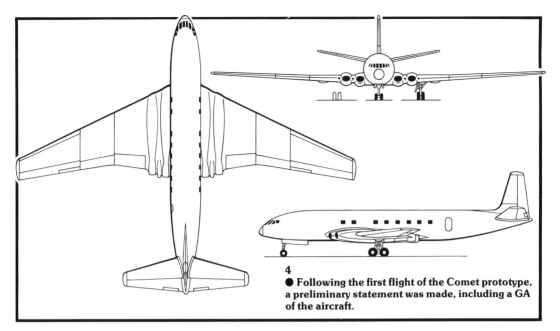

4

● **Following the first flight of the Comet prototype, a preliminary statement was made, including a GA of the aircraft.**

excessive fuel consumption at low altitudes, the Comet would require prompt handling by air traffic control, particularly during bad weather conditions.

De Havilland could not build such a new concept in aviation transportation without close collaboration with the users of the aircraft to allow the evolution of a safe and dependable transport system. Practical airline experience had to be combined with airfield operations, and close consultation with the government establishments and airworthiness authorities to suit this whole new concept to commercial operations.

With an economic service ceiling of around 40,000ft, the air conditioning system had to provide demanding standards of comfort for the average passenger, who did not wish to have to pass a stringent medical or wear an oxygen mask. Not only was the cabin pressurised to 8.5lb/sq in, but the air conditioning would require cooling and heating elements, as well as humidifiers to supply the moisture not normally in the air at such high altitudes. The air was also to be changed every 3min. In fact, the cabin environment was one of the most demanding areas of technology to be overcome.

Left:
The Comet prototype was rolled out of the Experimental hangar on 2 April 1949, with only the port pair of Ghost engines fitted.

Right:
The Comet prototype with Class B markings, G-5-1, and external mass balances on the rudder and elevators.

The Comet was to have a flight crew of four and be able to carry up to 36 passengers in a high level of comfort, avoiding travel weariness over the relatively faster flight times anticipated.

An all-metal monoplane, the Comet was to have a modestly swept-back wing and a tricycle undercarriage with a steerable nosewheel. Pressure refuelling was specified to speed the turnround and uplift of the large amount of fuel. The fuel could be quickly jettisoned in an emergency. Power controls and an electronic autopilot would assist handling on long flights. The jet engines would also bring an improved simplicity of operations, when compared with the piston-engined propeller-driven airliners. The paraffin fuel was also much less of a fire hazard than petrol.

The four 5,000lb thrust Ghost engines were expected to give the Comet a cruising speed of 500mph, and the development of the new powerplants was proceeding satisfactorily in parallel with the new airframe.

Publicity barriers were down for the maiden flight of the de Havilland Comet on 27 July 1949, flown by John Cunningham on his 32nd birthday. The national and aviation press were invited to Hatfield to inspect the new aircraft on that day and see it taxying and making initial hops as it ran along the runway. In the evening, when the press had departed thinking all was finished for the day, the inspection department advised John Cunningham that the aircraft was ready. He decided to make the first flight immediately with John Wilson as second pilot, Frank Reynolds as flight engineer, assisted by Harry Waters looking after the electronics, and Tony Fairbrother as flight test observer. It was a long time before the press forgave de Havilland for not making the maiden flight publicly, but no initial flight can be made to a timetable.

The aircraft was airborne for 31min, flying to 10,000ft to check handling at low and medium speeds before making a flypast at Hatfield for a few hundred employees who had heard of the flight and had come to watch the return.

In the first 18 working days, the Comet prototype completed 32.5hr of test-flying, achieving operational speeds and altitudes and had covered all the general handling at medium loadings. Handling was found to be satisfactory in the air and on the ground. The excellent serviceability of both the airframe and engines enabled the aircraft to operate up to four and five flights daily with only refuelling and modest attention. The aircraft was now ready for its complete programme of development trials, to investigate its full performance and operating envelope.

In keeping with the de Havilland philosophy over many years, the external shape of the Comet was designed to produce as little drag as possible, by careful attention to detail. The Ghost engines were buried in the wing root within the depth of a relatively thin wing, and the air intake was through the front spar of the wing, the low weight of the engines giving a good power-to-weight ratio. The close working relationship between the airframe and engine design teams was found to be essential for success. The air intakes and exhaust had to be precisely optimised for the engine to gain the maximum performance, or the refinements developed by the Ghost designers could be completely wasted. The absence of propellers allowed a short undercarriage, reducing weight in the units and surrounding structure. To help maintain structural strength — low weight, while also reducing drag — much of the fuselage and wing skinning was assembled by Redux bonding, or cementing metal to metal, instead of riveting. This was particularly useful for the attachment of stringers and stiffeners to the skins.

In October 1949, de Havilland revealed further information of the philosophy of the aircraft and

details of its internal layout. Although flight development was obviously progressing well, there was a reluctance to divulge any estimated performance figures until they were known more precisely. One important point had emerged from studies, confirmed by flight testing, and that was the Comet was not just a long-range aircraft, but could perform well on intercity routes of less than 1,000 miles, where the speed could still give a useful time-saving. On shorter-range operations, the reduction in fuel load would allow a greater payload capacity. The simplicity of jet operations also brought additional economic advantages and an airline would have the advantage of a common aircraft serving a greater proportion of the overall route structure.

Many advantages were brought by the jet engine: the simplicity gave durability and weight saving, particularly with the reduction in the usual ancillaries associated with piston engines. Engine life would be extended and servicing would be easier. The jet engine provided rapid start-up in cold weather, with no warm-up period, it was more accessible due to the short undercarriage and a Ghost engine could be changed in one hour.

Sufficient surplus power was developed by the jet engine to provide compressed air for cabin pressurisation, avoiding the weight and complication of a separate compressor system and adequate heat was available for cabin warmth and airframe de-icing. Compared with current piston-engined transport aircraft, the cockpit controls and instrumentation were very much simpler, reflecting the whole concept of the Comet and its operations: it would not require a team of supermen to operate this new system.

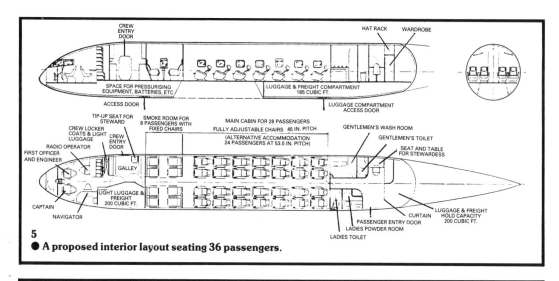

5
● **A proposed interior layout seating 36 passengers.**

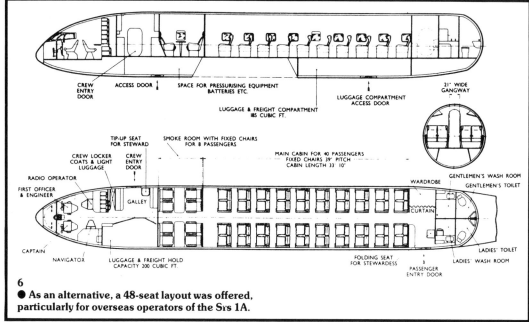

6
● **As an alternative, a 48-seat layout was offered, particularly for overseas operators of the Srs 1A.**

The 36 passengers were arranged in two cabins, eight forward of the front spar structural bulkhead with fixed chairs facing each other across fixed tables and the remaining 28 to the rear. The rear cabin was equipped with fully adjustable seats in seven rows of four, two abreast on either side of a central aisle, at a generous 45in pitch. The central gangway was 17in wide with a 6ft 5½in minimum headroom. A wardrobe for passengers' coats was located adjacent to the main entry door, and 200cu ft of space was available in the cabin for passengers' carry-on luggage.

Passengers entered and left the aircraft through a door in the rear port side of the cabin, while crew, galley and forward freight hold access was through a door in the forward starboard section of the cabin. All access doors and escape hatches in the pressure cabin were inward-opening plug-type. A galley was located at the forward end of the cabin, and separate ladies' and gentlemen's toilets were proposed. A total capacity of 585cu ft was available for mail, freight and luggage, both above and below the cabin floor, all within the pressure shell.

The aircrew of four consisted of captain, first officer, radio officer and navigator. Navigation equipment consisted of Loran, DME, ADF, ILS, ORB, G IV B compass and radio altimeter. All radio and navigation system aerials were suppressed into

The Simple Cockpit of the Comet

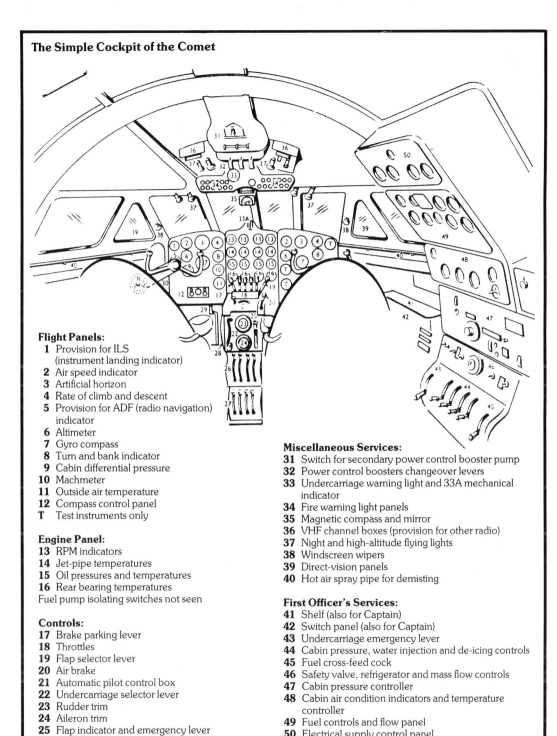

Flight Panels:
1 Provision for ILS
  (instrument landing indicator)
2 Air speed indicator
3 Artificial horizon
4 Rate of climb and descent
5 Provision for ADF (radio navigation)
  indicator
6 Altimeter
7 Gyro compass
8 Turn and bank indicator
9 Cabin differential pressure
10 Machmeter
11 Outside air temperature
12 Compass control panel
T Test instruments only

Engine Panel:
13 RPM indicators
14 Jet-pipe temperatures
15 Oil pressures and temperatures
16 Rear bearing temperatures
Fuel pump isolating switches not seen

Controls:
17 Brake parking lever
18 Throttles
19 Flap selector lever
20 Air brake
21 Automatic pilot control box
22 Undercarriage selector lever
23 Rudder trim
24 Aileron trim
25 Flap indicator and emergency lever
26 High-pressure fuel cocks
27 Low-pressure fuel cocks
28 Elevator trim wheel (also for First Officer)
29 Adjustment for rudder (toe-brake) pedals
30 Captain's control column and steering wheel

Miscellaneous Services:
31 Switch for secondary power control booster pump
32 Power control boosters changeover levers
33 Undercarriage warning light and 33A mechanical
  indicator
34 Fire warning light panels
35 Magnetic compass and mirror
36 VHF channel boxes (provision for other radio)
37 Night and high-altitude flying lights
38 Windscreen wipers
39 Direct-vision panels
40 Hot air spray pipe for demisting

First Officer's Services:
41 Shelf (also for Captain)
42 Switch panel (also for Captain)
43 Undercarriage emergency lever
44 Cabin pressure, water injection and de-icing controls
45 Fuel cross-feed cock
46 Safety valve, refrigerator and mass flow controls
47 Cabin pressure controller
48 Cabin air condition indicators and temperature
  controller
49 Fuel controls and flow panel
50 Electrical supply control panel

7

● **The Comet 1 flightdeck provided an improved
simplicity over the earlier more complex piston-
engined airliners.**

the structure to reduce drag. A Smith's SEP1 autopilot was fitted.

All flying controls were power-operated by duplicated hydraulic boosters. Split flaps were fitted on the inboard trailing edge of the wing with plain flaps outboard to the ailerons. Deceleration was achieved with air brakes on the wings, giving a high rate of descent without increased forward speed. There were no wing leading edge devices. All fuel was carried in the wing, contained in bag tanks in the centre section, and integral tanks outboard.

The Comet made its first public appearance at the Farnborough Air show in September 1949, where it was not only the flagship of the de Havilland exhibits but gave a glimpse into the future of air transport.

Such was the confidence in the test programme, that John Cunningham made the first overseas flight on 25 October 1949, only three months after its maiden flight to Castel Benito in Libya. The flight was made to and from Heathrow, the outbound journey taking 3hr 23min, giving an average speed of 440mph. On the return, 500 miles were covered in 61min, the total time being 3hr 45min at an average speed of 458mph. The cruising altitude had been 35,000ft.

Meanwhile, the routine development programme had included flights of up to 5½hr duration, a Mach number above 0.8 was measured in a shallow dive, and an altitude of 43,000ft was reached. The 375 miles from Edinburgh to Brighton were flown in 42min, averaging 530mph, and during a flight of 5hr 35min on 14 November at up to 40,000ft, the

590 miles from Shetland to Hatfield were clocked in 60min. The high level of serviceability of the new prototype was good enough to permit an average of over one hour's flying during its first 110 days.

Following the first four to five months of development flying, certain definite trends were emerging to make the Comet highly competitive in the world markets. The higher operating speeds made the aircraft 20% cheaper per ton-mile, and also enabled the aircraft to fly half as much again as conventional aircraft, resulting in increased earnings in proportion. Further improvements were anticipated with continuing developments.

Performance figures established included a cruising speed of 490mph at heights up to 40,000ft. At an all-up weight of 105,000lb and a capacity payload as a 36-seater of 12,000lb, the ultimate

still-air range was 3,540 statute miles. With full diversion allowances, this range became a more practical 2,654 miles. With full fuel tanks the ultimate still-air range rose to 2,920 miles, but with the payload reduced to 8,850lb. For delivery flights without payload, the range could be up to 3,220 miles, an increase achieved due to the reduced all-up weight.

With the all-up weight of 105,000lb, runway lengths of 2,175yd were required and normal operational stage lengths would be 2,140 miles allowing fully for diversions and reserves. The

Below:
The Comet prototype being prepared for engine runs.

interest in North Atlantic operations allowed the Comet to fly the most demanding Prestwick to Gander crossing of 2,116 miles with a 50% regularity according to wind strength, carrying a payload of 8,750lb. This allowed for a 395-mile diversion to Goose Bay, but of course did not give the Comet a nonstop capability between the major business destinations of London and New York. That was to come later, although in-flight refuelling was considered for the Comet, no doubt to some discomfort for the passengers due to the manoeuvring required to maintain contact with the tanker. Even with the technical stops at Prestwick and Gander, the Comet reduced transatlantic flight times westbound from 18 to 12hr and eastbound from 12½ to 9hr.

In a high-density 48-seat layout with a payload capacity of 14,000lb, the Comet could operate stage lengths of 1,750 miles from 2,000yd runways. To assist in hot and high take-offs, provision was made for a pair of Sprite rockets to be located between each pair of the Ghost engine jet pipes. Although this installation was tested as part of the development programme, it was never adopted in service, probably because of safety factors on the ground and in the air. Also, Ghost engine development was promising more thrust and lower fuel consumption. Other improvements anticipated were an increase in the all-up weight and the internal fuel capacity.

From its first flight in July, to the end of December 1949, the Comet prototype had flown 153.5hr in

Below left:
Compass swing of the Comet prototype in preparation for flight.

Centre left:
A series of low and high-speed taxi runs were made on the first prototype prior to the maiden flight.

Bottom left:
The Comet prototype lifts off from Hatfield in the early evening of 27 July 1949, captained by John Cunningham.

Right:
John Cunningham and the crew were congratulated by the team who had built the first prototype.

121 flights, the relative simplicity of the aircraft and its systems bringing the bonus of more flying for less maintenance. The basic price of a fully equipped and furnished Comet 1 was quoted at £450,000, but without the operator-specified radio equipment. The major external difference between the two prototypes and series production was the single large mainwheel on the test aircraft being replaced by a more practical four-wheel bogie assembly for commercial service.

To prepare for anticipated large volume orders, de Havilland doubled its floor space by taking over the Vickers wartime factory at Hawarden near Chester. Initially, Comet production was located at Hatfield, with all the other aircraft such as Vampire, Hornet, Mosquito and Chipmunk being built at Chester. The production area was also large enough for a second Comet line when demand outgrew the Hatfield factory.

As a justification for providing increased production capability, Canadian Pacific Air Lines (CPA) announced on 15 December 1949 the first export order for two Comets in the 48-seat configuration, with more aircraft expected to be added later. CPA planned to use the aircraft from Vancouver to Hong Kong, staging through Anchorage, Shemya beyond the Aleutian Island chain, and Tokyo. This routeing went a quarter of the way around the world over some of the most remote areas, in 20hr including stops. The Comets were ordered to replace Canadair DC-4s on the Oriental route, and to expand the international CPA services around and across the Pacific. The Rolls-Royce Merlin-powered Canadair 4s were taking about 45hr to fly the Orient route westbound compared with the Comet's 20hr, and the 38hr eastbound flight schedule was reduced to around 15hr in the Comet. The maximum stage was 2,040 statute miles from Shemya to Tokyo.

As the test-flying progressed and improvements were incorporated, comparisons could be made with other conventional forms of transport to demonstrate the advantages of higher speeds. With an annual utilisation of 2,550hr, a fleet of nine Comets could carry as many passengers as Cunard's *Queen Elizabeth* ocean liner over the same period.

The normal capacity of the *Queen Elizabeth* was 2,200 passengers and it could make the round trip between 40 and 45 times in the year. The Comet could carry 36 passengers on average 300 times in a year, covering a very low utilisation of six single

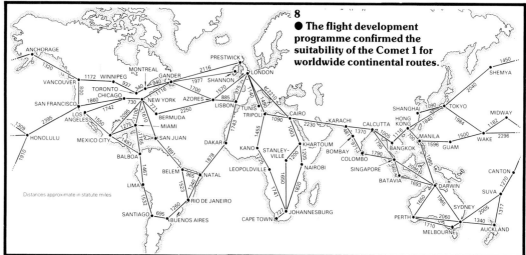

8
● **The flight development programme confirmed the suitability of the Comet 1 for worldwide continental routes.**

Distances approximate in statute miles

weekly trips from London to New York in 12hr and 9hr back. The ocean liner required about five days either way, which is fine for a relaxing cruise in good weather.

The passenger appeal of the Comet pioneered the standards now considered normal and routine. The greater altitudes flown took the aircraft into smoother air above the weather and removed sensation of speed. The absence of vibration and dramatic reduction in noise not only improved comfort, but reduced fatigue on arrival at the destination.

By March 1950, the second prototype was in final assembly in the main erecting shop at Hatfield, with the first four production aircraft for BOAC taking shape behind. In the same month, the Comet

Top:
Even the underside of the Comet presented a clean low-drag shape.

prototype gained four inter-capital records, out and back to Rome and Copenhagen. Everywhere the Comet flew it established new rapid times. On 16 March, Hatfield to Rome was flown in 2hr 2min 52sec, achieving a speed of 447.246mph. The return took nearly two more minutes, reducing the average speed to 442.326mph. The record was based on the equivalent city centre-to-city centre times of 1hr 59min 37sec, and 2hr 57sec respectively. On 21 March, Hatfield to Copenhagen was flown in 1hr 18min 36.5sec, and the return in

1hr 24min 52sec. The average speeds were 453.98mph and 420.36mph.

A month later the Comet prototype left Hatfield for tropical trials in Africa to prove performance at high temperatures and high altitudes. On the outbound flight from Hatfield to Cairo on 24 April, it flew the 2,182 miles in just on 5hr 9min, clocking an average of 426.63mph. The next day the 2,195 miles from Cairo to Nairobi was flown in 5hr 15min giving a speed of around 420mph. The aircraft carried the equivalent of a load of 34 passengers and their baggage out of the restricted Hatfield runway.

Nairobi presented the most demanding part of the performance testing, at an altitude of 5,370ft above sea level and temperatures equivalent to 34°C or 93°F. Khartoum was used for the higher temperature, lower altitude performance testing, the Comet returning to Hatfield on 11 May.

On the first anniversary of the maiden flight of the first Comet, the second aircraft, G-ALZK, joined the test programme. The crew were John Cunningham as captain, Peter Bugge as second pilot, E. Brackstone Brown — better known as Brax — as flight engineer and K. G. Rendle monitoring the test instrumentation. The polished metal second prototype was airborne for 28min and still featured the large single mainwheel undercarriage. The four-wheel production unit was tested on the first prototype, but there was insufficient room in the wing for it to retract until modifications were made for the production aircraft.

At the Farnborough Air Show in September 1950, the first prototype appeared in the full airline livery of BOAC, while the first aircraft for the airline were in advanced stage of assembly on the Hatfield production line.

The first production Comet 1, G-ALYP, joined

Top:
Sprite rocket engines were tested on the Comet prototype to boost performance during hot and high take-offs.

Right:
Although the first prototype Comet was built in the Experimental hangar, all subsequent aircraft, including the second prototype, were built in the main assembly hall on production jigs.

the development programme on 9 January 1951, by which time the prototypes had flown over 525hr, the first aircraft concentrating on aerodynamics and performance testing while the second prototype concentrated on systems development. On completion of the maker's tests, the second prototype was delivered to BOAC for route proving of this new concept in air transport. It arrived at London's Heathrow Airport on 2 April 1951 to begin a programme of exploration of jet airliner operating techniques in preparation for the delivery of the first service aircraft later in the year. Amongst areas to be studied was the effect on air traffic control, high altitude meteorological studies over the BOAC worldwide route structure, the measurement of cruise economy and performance, and the checking of the radio and navigation aids. The programme was compiled and monitored in co-operation with the airworthiness authorities, who were involved with setting the new standards of safe operation.

During the first eight weeks with BOAC the Comet flew 147hr, initially around the UK for performance measuring, but then extending out on the route structure to Cairo, Calcutta and further

afield. No passengers were carried as the aircraft interior was not representative and was not fully furnished.

In the spring of 1951, two Comet 1s were ordered by the French company Chargeurs Réunis SA of Paris, to be operated by its associate airline, the independent Union Aéromaritime de Transport (UAT). The aircraft, due for delivery at the end of 1952, were ordered for the Paris to Africa routes including Casablanca, Dakar, Abidjan, Bamako, Duala and Brazzaville. The Comets were also to be flown on the eastern route to Saigon. The average stage lengths in Africa were 1,400 to 1,800 miles with some as short as 650 miles. The UAT Comets

Above left:
Exactly one year after the maiden flight of the first Comet, John Cunningham made the first flight in the second prototype, G-ALZK, on 27 July 1950.

Left:
As part of the testing of the production main undercarriage, the four-wheel bogie units were fitted to the first prototype, although they could not be retracted.

Bottom:
In September 1950 the first prototype Comet was demonstrated at Farnborough.

were furnished with 44 seats and had a capacity payload of 13,500lb, making them highly competitive with the existing aircraft.

As the overseas proving flights progressed, seats were fitted in the cabin to accommodate the VIP passengers who helped promote the Comet at the overseas destinations where it created so much interest. One of these flights in the series was London to Johannesburg on 17-18 July 1951. The flight via Cairo and Entebbe took a total of 17hr 33min to cover the 6,212 miles, of which 15hr 9min were the time in the air. Passengers could complete a day's work in London, fly overnight to Johannesburg and arrive in time for lunch the next day, without being exhausted from the journey. This operation was a rehearsal for regular joint operations by BOAC and South African Airways known as the 'Springbok Service'. In two years of testing, more than 1,000hr had been

flown by four Comets, with deliveries to BOAC imminent.

The production Comet 1s for BOAC were to carry 36 passengers with a generous 45in seat pitch. The cabins were furnished as one class, as is Concorde today — 28 people in the main cabin paired on either side of a 17in-wide aisle. The remaining eight passengers were in the forward cabin with facing seats separated by stowable tables, ideally for a group of travellers. These tables allowed restaurant-style meals to be served.

On 28 July 1951, the fourth Comet 1 joined the test programme, almost two years to the day after the maiden flight of the prototype, soon to be followed by the fifth aircraft. The second aircraft had covered some 45,000 miles on the route proving trials with BOAC.

In September 1951, Canadian Pacific announced its decision to allocate its Comets to its South Pacific

Above left:
The two Comet prototypes shared the bulk of the flight test programme.

Left:
The first overseas order for the Comet came from Canadian Pacific and the expanding sales required the construction of a new flight test hangar at Hatfield.

Below left:
First production Comet 1 for BOAC, G-ALYP, 'Yoke-Peter', made its maiden flight on 9 January 1951.

Above:
Comet 1, G-ALYP, joined the two prototypes in the development programme to confirm the production standards of performance and economics.

routes, instead of from Vancouver to Tokyo and Hong Kong. The aircraft would therefore be on the Vancouver to Australia service, reducing the long travel times, with the Comet 1s covering the southern part of the routes from Honolulu. The Vancouver to Honolulu leg of 2,800 miles was better suited to the planned Comet 2, and would be flown in the meantime by DC-6Bs. The Comet 1s would therefore be based in Sydney, flying two round trips a week, one to Honolulu via Fiji and Canton, and the other including Auckland as an additional call. The longest stage was the 2,000 miles between Sydney and Fiji.

Meanwhile G-ALZK was continuing its worldwide proving flights, the tenth in the series being to Pakistan and India. The journey from London to Karachi took an elapsed time of 12hr 13min, arriving at 05.46 GMT on 31 August. The 4,545-mile flight included a 59min stop at Cairo. Although the flight was not timed for a record, it beat the previous best time, held by a single-seat fighter, by over 3hr.

On 30 October 1951, UAT increased its order for Comet 1s from two to three aircraft with options on the later, more powerful, Comet 2.

On 19 October 1951, G-ALZK landed at Heathrow at the end of the twelfth overseas tour, completing a six-month programme of over 460hr of flying under airline operating conditions. The Comet had flown over 91,000 miles, making 91 landings at 31 overseas airports. In addition to gaining data on long distance cruise techniques in all climates, traffic patterns were investigated at the major airports, including alternative approach procedures at Heathrow. Technical delays were minimal, and mainly cured by the normal network of spares provision around an established route network. As was to be expected, many fast times were clocked on the major routes.

As a result of the tests, it was shown that the Comet, even in its early undeveloped form, could fit into the route patterns with no difficulty, and was well suited to the airfield approach procedures without any penalty. Both the aircrew and ground crew found the Comet easy to operate with good serviceability and favourable handling. The fast, smooth over-the-weather flying was expected to make the Comet popular with its passengers.

The latter part of 1951 not only saw the sixth Comet, G-ALYU, into the air on 31 December, but also news of significant new sales. British Commonwealth Pacific Airlines (BCPA), a company jointly owned by the governments of Britain, Australia and New Zealand, announced in Sydney at the end of the year that approval had been given to order six

Comet jet airliners. These aircraft, to replace DC-6s on the transpacific routes connecting the Antipodes with North America, were to be the longer range Comet 2 development, powered by four Rolls-Royce Avon axial-flow jet engines. The prototype of this version had started engine runs at Hatfield on 1 January 1952. The six 44-seat BCPA Comets were due for delivery in 1954-55, and the initial value without spares was £3 million. The flight time over the 7,500 miles of ocean, with three stops, was expected to take 10hr off the total journey time.

Air France announced approval for three Comet 1s on 21 November 1951 for operation on its long-range trunk routes from Paris to Cairo,

Beirut, and Dakar, and an express service to Saigon. Other destinations being considered were an extension of the Dakar route to Buenos Aires with Comet 2s, and Paris to Brazzaville across the Sahara desert replacing Lockheed Constellations. Deliveries were expected to commence in 1953.

A military order came from the Royal Canadian Air Force for two Series 1 Comets for high speed communications, as well as simulating attacks from high speed, high altitude jet bombers to test Canada's defences.

The orders brought the sales and commitments to a total of 45 Comets, of which 21 were Comet 1s, and 24 Series 2s, including the original two prototypes.

On 22 January 1952, de Havilland Comet 1, G-ALYS, became the world's first commercial jet airliner, when its Certificate of Airworthiness was awarded allowing it to enter worldwide service, years ahead of any competition. The aim of being ahead of the American aircraft industry had been achieved.

Left:
The world's first jet transport Certificate of Airworthiness was awarded to the Comet on 22 January 1952.

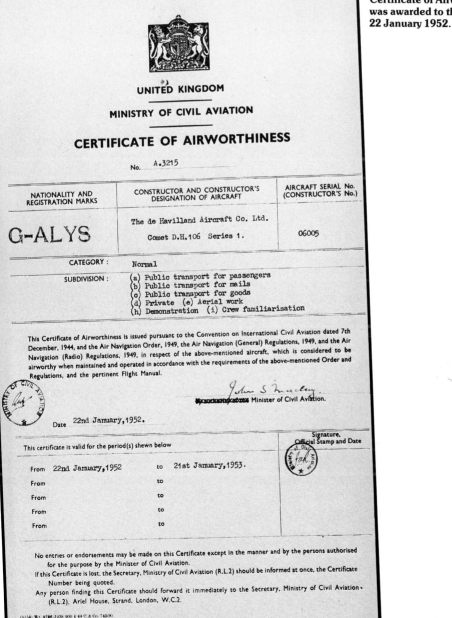

M.C.A. Form No. 958

UNITED KINGDOM

MINISTRY OF CIVIL AVIATION

CERTIFICATE OF AIRWORTHINESS

No. A.3215

NATIONALITY AND REGISTRATION MARKS	CONSTRUCTOR AND CONSTRUCTOR'S DESIGNATION OF AIRCRAFT	AIRCRAFT SERIAL No. (CONSTRUCTOR'S No.)
G-ALYS	The de Havilland Aircraft Co. Ltd. Comet D.H.106 Series 1.	06005

CATEGORY :	Normal
SUBDIVISION :	(a) Public transport for passengers (b) Public transport for mails (c) Public transport for goods (d) Private (e) Aerial work (h) Demonstration (i) Crew familiarisation

This Certificate of Airworthiness is issued pursuant to the Convention on International Civil Aviation dated 7th December, 1944, and the Air Navigation Order, 1949, the Air Navigation (General) Regulations, 1949, and the Air Navigation (Radio) Regulations, 1949, in respect of the above-mentioned aircraft, which is considered to be airworthy when maintained and operated in accordance with the requirements of the above-mentioned Order and Regulations, and the pertinent Flight Manual.

John S Maclay.
Minister of Civil Aviation.

Date 22nd January, 1952.

This certificate is valid for the period(s) shewn below

Signature, Official Stamp and Date

From	22nd January, 1952	to	21st January, 1953.
From		to	
From		to	
From		to	
From		to	

No entries or endorsements may be made on this Certificate except in the manner and by the persons authorised for the purpose by the Minister of Civil Aviation.

If this Certificate is lost, the Secretary, Ministry of Civil Aviation (R.L.2) should be informed at once, the Certificate Number being quoted.

Any person finding this Certificate should forward it immediately to the Secretary, Ministry of Civil Aviation, (R.L.2), Ariel House, Strand, London, W.C.2.

(9158) Wt. 9786 J 938 900 4 49 C.& Co. 745(8)

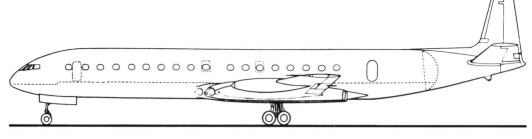

Service Entry and Developments

With a Certificate of Airworthiness awarded, deliveries of Comet 1s commenced to BOAC at Heathrow. The first to arrive was G-ALYS on 4 February 1952, handed over six months ahead of contract date by John Cunningham to Capt A. M. Majendie, for crew training and route-proving to commence. The arrival of G-ALYU and G-ALYP on 6 and 13 March allowed preparations to be made for the world's first commercial jet passenger service on 2 May, leaving London for Johannesburg.

Meanwhile the development Comet 2, G-ALYT, adapted from a Series 1 in the BOAC batch, flew for the first time from Hatfield on 16 February 1952,

powered by four Rolls-Royce Avon engines, developing 6,500lb thrust each. John Cunningham headed the crew for this nearly 2hr initial flight at heights of up to 25,000ft.

The slim Avons fitted easily into the existing engine bays with minor alterations to the wing structure, but the increased thrust required larger intakes for the greater volume of air, and larger jet

Below:
Flightdeck layout and crew apparel have changed somewhat since the start of the commercial jet age.

pipes. The increased thrust also allowed a greater payload of up to 44 passengers, and greater fuel load to improve range. BOAC was launch customer for 11 of this new version, followed by BCPA.

Above:
BOAC accepted its first Comet 1, G-ALYS, at London's Heathrow Airport on 31 January 1952.

Below:
The Rolls-Royce Avon engines for the prototype Comet 2, G-ALYT.

Early in March 1952, total flying time on the Comets passed 2,000hr, all on test, development, route-proving and crew training, over half the hours being accumulated by the two prototypes. Meanwhile, to keep pace with anticipated demand de Havilland announced an agreement with Short Brothers to manufacture Comets at Belfast. This would in effect double the production capacity, the first Short-built aircraft emerging in 1954.

As planned, passenger services commenced on 2 May 1952, with the departure of G-ALYP, the first production Comet 1, from runway 10(R) at Heathrow, heading for Johannesburg. In command

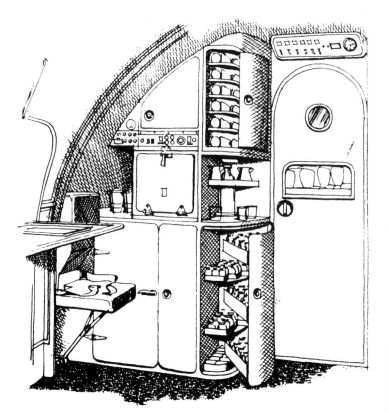

of this flight was Capt Majendie, carrying 30 passengers on the 23hr 37min journey. The return was made by departing on the morning of 5 May, arriving 22hr 48min later at Heathrow.

The initial plan was to operate a once-a-week round trip to Johannesburg, but because of the increased demand, the service was trebled within one month of the start. The Comets operated the Springbok route in conjunction with South African Airways, and the new jets progressively replaced Handley Page Hermes flying down the east side of Africa. Plans were also in hand to start services to Singapore later in the year, with route-proving flights commencing on 15 May.

In contrast to the world's first jet passenger service, de Havilland had played a significant part in early commercial aviation. It was a DH4A of Air Transport and Travel which inaugurated the world's first international air service on 25 August 1919 from London to Paris. The average flying time for the 240-mile route was 2hr 30min. The passengers were accommodated in a small cabin, while the pilot was exposed to the elements in a cockpit under the wing centre-section.

Within three months of the ratification of the Peace Treaty between Japan and the Allies, de Havilland was able to announce orders for Comets, Herons and Doves to help Japan's airline industry. Japan Airlines ordered two Comet 2s to restart its international routes to Europe and across the Pacific. The arrival of BOAC Comet 1, G-ALYP, on 8 July 1952 on the first of its proving flights, created a great deal of interest in the aircraft.

Two Comet 2s were ordered by LAV of Venezuela to provide an express service from Caracas to New York, a distance of 2,410 miles in a time of 4hr 30min. The Comets were expected to replace Constellations in mid-1955.

The first export Comet, CF-CUM for Canadian Pacific, was redesignated Comet Series 1A, with an increased fuel capacity, increased all-up weight to 110,000lb, and water-methanol injection for the engines giving some 10% increase in take-off thrust. The 1,000Imp gal increase in fuel capacity, over the 6,000gal in the basic Comet 1, allowed the aircraft to be operated on 20% longer stage lengths. All the subsequent export Comet 1s were completed to the Series 1A standard.

BOAC continued to take delivery of its aircraft, the seventh – G-ALYX – being handed over at Heathrow on 23 July 1952. The airline also announced plans to commence regular Comet schedules to Asia, commencing on 11 August to Colombo, extending to Singapore in September.

At the Farnborough Air Show in September 1952, the Canadian Pacific Comet 1A CF-CUM was exhibited, and future developments of the Comet family were revealed. Only 21 of the Comet Srs 1

and 1A were to be built, followed by the 44-seat more powerful and longer range Comet 2 for delivery from 1954 onwards. The new development announced was the 58-78 passenger Comet 3 available from 1957. The enlarged Comet 3, which was in an advanced design stage, was to have an all-up weight of 145,000lb. Increased power would come from four improved Avon engines developing 9,000lb of thrust each, and giving a cruising speed of over 500mph. Seating could be for 58 first class passengers, 78 tourist class, or any convenient combination. Stage lengths would be about 60% greater than the Comet 1 with much lower operating costs. It was expected that the prototype

Above:
The sixth Comet airframe, G-ALYT, was converted on the production line to the Mk 2 prototype, powered by four Rolls-Royce Avon engines in place of the Ghosts.

Right:
Comet services to Johannesburg were operated in conjunction with South African Airways.

The BOAC Comet services to
Tokyo were commenced on
2 April 1953 with Comet 1,
G-ALYX. *BOAC*

10
● After one year in service, Comets were flying 370hr a week over 122,000 miles. A total of 20,780 unduplicated miles was being flown at a profit.

LONDON
2.35
ROME
3.30
3.25
BEIRUT
CAIRO
2.55
2.50
3.05
BAHREIN
KHARTOUM
2.55
2.55
ENTEBBE
3.30
LIVINGSTONE
1.50
JOHANNESBURG

ELAPSED TIME 21 HOURS
20 MINUTES FROM LONDON

KARACHI
2.05
DELHI
2.20
CALCUTTA
3.40
1.50
BOMBAY
2.05
2.55
RANGOON
1.20
BANGKOK
3.50
3.25
2.40
2.50
COLOMBO

ELAPSED TIME
20 HOURS 35 MINUTES
FROM LONDON

SINGAPORE
ELAPSED TIME
25 HOURS 30 MINUTES
FROM LONDON

ELAPSED TIME
36 HOURS 20 MINUTES
FROM LONDON
TOKYO
2.50
OKINAWA
2.45
MANILA

Top:
The Canadian Pacific Comet, CF-CUM, was the first of the improved Srs 1A versions with higher all-up weight.

Right:
BOAC Comet 1, G-ALYY, was used for route-proving to Asia. It was later lost off Stromboli on 8 April 1954.

The BOAC Comet 1 fleet was completed with the delivery of G-ALYZ on 30 September 1952.

of this new stretched version would fly in early 1954, followed by the first production aircraft in late 1956.

BOAC Comet 1, G-ALYU, operated the first weekly service from London to Colombo on 11 August 1952, covering the 5,925 miles in a total elapsed time of 21hr 35min. Stops were made at Rome, Beirut, Bahrain, Karachi and Bombay. The service on to Singapore was planned to commence on 14 October in an elapsed time of 27½hr; a further extension to Tokyo was planned for early 1953. All nine Comet 1s had been delivered to BOAC, the last, G-ALYZ, handed over on 30 September, with Comet 2 deliveries expected to commence at the end of 1953. The Comet 1s were profitable on the BOAC routes.

More details on the Comet 3 were revealed in December 1952, the 18ft stretched fuselage accommodating 58 first class passengers in a four-abreast layout, while the tourist seating was five-abreast. Additional fuel was carried in pinion tanks fitted to the wing leading edges, about two-thirds of the way from the fuselage to the wing-tip. Both wing and flap area was increased, overall fuel capacity being increased to over 6,000gal. Many other improvements were being progressively introduced into both the Comet 2 and later the Comet 3, as experience was gained in airline operation. The Comet 3 was designed for a practical stage length with a 17,450lb payload of 2,700 miles. This made the aircraft suitable for many of the longer routes, but on the initial westerly flight from London to New York, one intermediate stop was required with capacity payload and full fuel reserves.

The Comet had achieved such an excellent reputation, that Pan American became the first American airline to order a British aircraft. On 20 October 1952 it was announced that Pan Am had ordered three of the new Comet 3s for delivery in 1956 and with options on a further seven for delivery the following year. BOAC had already decided to acquire 11 Comet 3s, but agreed to release three of its early aircraft, to meet the delivery schedules of Pan Am, making it the first US operator of jet airliners.

The first major incident happened to BOAC Comet 1, G-ALYZ, at Rome on 26 October 1952, when the aircraft failed to take off. The aircraft ran off the end of the runway into soft ground, removing the undercarriage and rupturing the integral wing fuel tanks. There was no fire and all the occupants of the aircraft were unhurt. In a preliminary statement by the Chief Inspector of Accidents, there was no failure of the aircraft or its engines. However, subsequent events were to prove slightly different.

When the report was published, the cause of the accident was attributed to pilot error. It was stated that the aircraft acceleration did not build up normally, due to the progressive nose-up attitude on take-off. This phenomena was a new one experienced with the low drag of the jet airliners, without the extra lift generated by propeller wash across the wings, It was to take another similar accident before corrections were made to the wing profile to avoid stalling the aircraft during the take-off run. Now all airliners have to demonstrate that they can take off safely even with the tail skid dragging along the runway.

The first export Comet 1A delivery was F-BGSA to UAT at Le Bourget on 17 December 1952, and it soon commenced route-proving and crew training flights to West Africa in preparation for the start of regular jet operations in the spring of 1953.

Following the sale to LAV in Venezuela, Panair de Brasil ordered four Comet 2s with options on two Comet 3s at the end of 1952. The Comet 2s were to be the standard 44-seat version operating stage lengths of over 2,000 miles, in some cases way above the highest 20,000ft peaks of the Andes mountains. This brought total confirmed sales to 46 Comets with more than 100 potential sales for Comet 2s and 3s under active discussion.

With delivery of the second UAT Comet 1A, F-BGSB, on 19 February 1953, the aircraft entered

regular service with the airline, initially on the Paris-Casablanca-Dakar route.

On 26 January 1953, BCPA confirmed its order for three Comet 2s for delivery by the end of 1954. The original plan was to order six Comets, but with the availability of the Comet 3, the airline needed to determine its best future fleet mix. BOAC also extended operations by introducing the Comet to its Tokyo route on 3 April. The 10,000-mile route would be covered in just over 33hr, compared with the 86hr of the existing schedule. The initial service was once a week, but by midway through the month, two a week were operated.

The first fatal accident to a Comet was a repeat of the Rome accident. On this occasion, it was the delivery flight of CPA Comet 1A, CF-CUN, which failed to become airborne from Karachi on 2 March 1953, while en route to its planned operating base at Sydney. All the 11 occupants were killed in this ground stall accident, which clearly demonstrated a need for suitable safety modifications. The pioneering work of de Havilland had highlighted a previously unknown problem, which was to benefit worldwide jet airliner operations. The remaining CPA Comet 1A, CF-CUM, was not delivered to the airline, which changed its operating plans, and the aircraft joined BOAC as G-ANAV, its sole Comet 1A.

At 14.00hrs GMT, on 2 May 1953, BOAC completed the first year of commercial jet airliner operations, but this significant achievement was marred 2hr before by the loss of Comet 1, G-ALYV. The aircraft had taken off from Calcutta, heading eventually for London, when at around 10,000ft altitude, it had entered a violent storm with cumulo-nimbus thunder clouds, heavy turbulence and lightning. As a result of the high structural loads, the aircraft broke up in the air, killing all 37 passengers and six crew. The Comet was not fitted with weather radar to warn of storm clouds which should be avoided, since this was a subsequent addition to the navigational aids of commercial aircraft. No aircraft can reasonably be expected to survive in such turbulent conditions and, therefore, the Comet was not displaying any inherent weakness of the structure.

However, on the positive side, the first year of Comet operations had shown a profit over 9,000 revenue hours and 100 million passenger miles. The aircraft were operating on routes to Johannes-burg, Colombo, Singapore and Tokyo, flying 370hr and 122,000 miles every week. The total distances covered were 20,780 of unduplicated route miles, offering 4 million passenger-miles per week. During the year nearly 28,000 passengers were carried on the Comets. Such was the ease of operation of the aircraft that transit times were reduced from an initial 1hr to 40min.

All this was achieved with a fleet of eight Comet 1s, which were basic undeveloped aircraft, the experience gained allowing significant improvements to be incorporated into later versions. Both BOAC and de Havilland shared closely in the lessons learned from this invaluable operational experience of a new generation of air transportation.

Passenger appeal had been high, with an average 87% load factor for the year, not just for the novelty factor, but for the reduced journey times, smoothness and comfort.

A high proportion of the first year's flying had to be dedicated to route-proving and crew training, each captain having to complete 60hr of flying the Comet. This high level of training, which was before the development of today's sophisticated simulators, included about 10hr of conversion training, followed by at least two trips under supervision, of the route the pilot was to operate. By the end of the first year the target of 40 fully-operational crews was achieved, and further crews had already started their preparation for the introduction of the longer range Comet 2.

Not only had the Comets operated with few of the expected problems, but its operational flexibility was far higher than predicted with stage lengths varying from 1hr 20min from Rangoon to Bangkok, and 3hr 50min from Bangkok to Manila. It was found that operationally it fitted in well with existing airport procedures, including the busy Heathrow with its variable weather conditions. The rapid starting of the engines and lack of warm-up time normally required by piston engines, allowed the aircraft to obtain its flight clearance before engine start, and taxi rapidly to the take-off point for departure, reducing wasteful fuel consumption on the ground. The climb gradient to economic altitudes was well in excess of piston-engined aircraft, and once at altitude it could cruise at between 35,000 and 42,000ft, depending upon stage length, as the weight decreased with burning of the fuel.

Without the modern inertial navigation equipment, the Comet had a radio operator/navigator as part of the crew. The higher operating speeds of the aircraft required a more demanding rate of navigation to allow the captain to make decisions in advance and also to fit rapidly into airport let-down patterns to conserve fuel. The Comets were also flying in totally new meteorological conditions where lessons had to be learned about high level winds, and how to provide reliable forecasts.

The utilisation of the Comet fleet had been good with a level of 6½hr per day being achieved after the year's operation. Taking into account the relatively short stages, compared with today's long-range jets, the utilisation was probably more comparable with today's inter-European or domestic USA routes where a higher proportion of the working day is spent transiting airports. Also by the end of the first year the time lost by mechanical delays had been reduced to 9%.

Mechanical faults with the aircraft were relatively minor and easy to overcome. The hydraulics caused some early problems with regular airline usage, but after the first couple of months were largely rectified. The misting of the windscreen in high humidity conditions required more warm air to be blown across the inside of the glass and the original windscreen wiper was unable to cope with

the amount of rain experienced. Both comparatively minor problems, but vital to safety for the crews' clarity of vision. Despite the man-hours required for a Major Check 4 routine inspection being higher than predicted, they were still a significant improvement over even the best of the four-engined piston aircraft in the BOAC fleet. The overall high reliability had allowed the Check 4 to be progressively extended from an initially cautious 200hr to 1,040hr.

Engine problems were relatively minor with some cracking in the centrifugal compressor due to high frequency vibration, but cropping of the impeller blades removed it from the initial frequency range. The engines had entered service with a 250hr overhaul life, and finished the year with the imminent approval for 600hr between overhaul with flame tube inspections at 200hr. All overhauls were completed by the de Havilland Engine Company, to obtain first hand experience of the engine performance in worldwide service. The running time with BOAC had exceeded any previous experience with gas turbine engines, some of the Ghosts having achieved nearly 2,000hr. The

major cause of damage was foreign objects hitting the turbine blades, with no cases of thermal stress or fatigue.

With the introduction of the Comet on the Tokyo service on 2 April 1953, the elapsed time was reduced from 86hr by Argonaut to a mere 36hr over the 10,000 miles. A major part of the reduction was the avoidance of two night stops, and following a number of route-proving flights, the Comets fitted in well with the varied traffic patterns, achieving rapid turnarounds to take the best advantage of the fast flight times.

The first Comet 1A for the RCAF, VC5301, made it maiden flight on 21 February 1953 and was accepted on 18 March when crew training commenced. The second aircraft, VC5302, was handed over at Hatfield on 13 April, and following the base training, route training took place along the BOAC Johannesburg and Singapore stages. The aircraft then left for Canada, VC5301 being the first jet transport to cross the North Atlantic, arriving on 29 May via Keflavik and Goose Bay and commenced service with No 412 (Transport) Squadron based at Uplands aerodrome near Ottawa.

In the spring of 1953, Air India exercised its options for two Comet 3s for delivery in 1957, to operate initially an express luxury service between India and Britain.

Although members of the British Royal Family had flown on the Comet for the experience of jet flight, both HM Queen Elizabeth, the Queen Mother and HRH the Princess Margaret, flew on Comet 1, G-ALYW, from Heathrow on 30 June 1953, to attend the Rhodes Centenary Celebrations in what is now known as Zimbabwe. The return in the same aircraft was on 17 July.

The first Comet 1A for UAT, F-BGSA, was used to train 10 complete crews with this pioneering, privately-owned French airline. Route-proving

Left:
With the delivery of Comet 1A, F-BGSB, to UAT in February 1953, regular commercial services commenced.

Below left:
Canadian Pacific Comet 1A, CF-CUN, was lost on its delivery flight when it failed to take off from Karachi on 2 March 1953.

Below:
The remaining CPA Comet 1A, CF-CUM, became the sole Srs 1A with BOAC as G-ANAV. It was later flown at Farnborough during the Comet accident investigation.

flights totalled 20hr, during which French certification was awarded. UAT also maintained the Comets, engines and much of the equipment itself, the airframe checks being on multiples of 60hr, starting with a Check 1 and finishing with a Check 4 at 720hr. The airline inaugurated Comet services on 19 February 1953 when F-BGSA left Paris for Dakar via Casablanca on the first of a twice-weekly service. On the same day, the second UAT Comet arrived, allowing a twice-weekly service to Casablanca to start on 14 March. With the delivery of the third Comet, F-BGSC, on 30 April, a once-a-week service was started to Brazzaville on 6 May. Stage lengths varied from 1,145 and 1,970 miles and weekly aircraft utilisation was averaging 97hr, equal to an annual utilisation of 1,680hr. Amongst the improvements of the Comet 1A was water injection for the engines which improved take-off performance from hot and high airfields, particularly during the middle of the day. The UAT Comet passengers were charged at the first class rate, which was 20% more than the tourist class fare, many of the passengers being French families on duty with commercial organisations in West Africa, returning to France for their annual leave.

With its fleet of three Comet 1As delivered, UAT was flying 37,000 miles each week from Paris and Marseilles to Abidjan, Douala and Brazzaville. The delivery of four Comet 2s would allow route extensions to Recife via Dakar, Johannesburg and Saigon. Seven times a week a Comet left France for destinations in French West Africa, UAT having followed BOAC as the second operator of jet airliners when its services commenced on 19 February 1953.

The introduction of the Comet 2s in 1954-55 was expected to improve on the existing services by reducing refuelling stops, and also to open up new routes.

In the autumn of 1953, de Havilland was able to issue details of the economics of the planned Comet 3. Not only would this aircraft benefit from the experience gained from the undeveloped Comet 1 in service with BOAC, but it could also take advantage of the rapid technological advances, particularly in respect of the more powerful and economic jet engines, since the Comet 1 was designed. The Comet 3 would have an increased passenger capacity over greater ranges, giving the aircraft a marked economic advantage over existing piston-engined airliners.

The 58 first class passengers or alternatively 70 tourist class passengers gave capacity payloads of 17,350lb or 20,000lb respectively. With the lower payload, the aircraft could fly 2,600-mile stage lengths from 7,000ft runways at sea level up to temperatures of 30°C, with normal provision for reserves. The corresponding ultimate range was

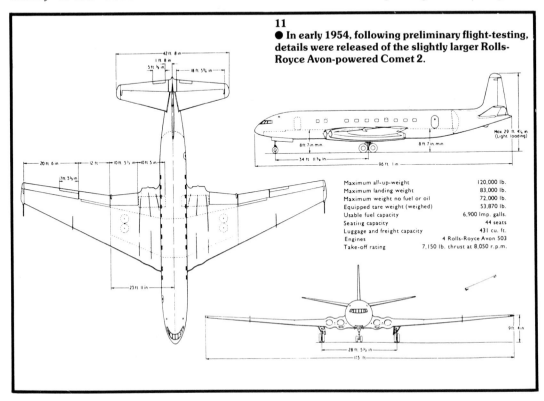

11
● In early 1954, following preliminary flight-testing, details were released of the slightly larger Rolls-Royce Avon-powered Comet 2.

Maximum all-up-weight	120,000 lb.
Maximum landing weight	83,000 lb.
Maximum weight no fuel or oil	72,000 lb.
Equipped tare weight (weighed)	53,870 lb.
Usable fuel capacity	6,900 Imp. galls.
Seating capacity	44 seats
Luggage and freight capacity	431 cu. ft.
Engines	4 Rolls-Royce Avon 503
Take-off rating	7,150 lb. thrust at 8,050 r.p.m.

4,250 miles. The tourist capacity payload could be carried on stage lengths of 2,400 miles under similar conditions, the ultimate range being 4,000 miles. This was achieved at a cruising speed of 500mph.

The Comet 3, taking advantage of its development potential, showed significant advances over existing piston-engined airliners. Despite much higher fuel consumption per hour, a slightly reduced payload, and a 50% greater first cost, the revenue earning ability of the Comet was 50% greater than the competition. As a result the Comet 3 provided 10% better value for money than the conventional piston-engined airliners.

In maintenance and overhaul terms, the costs of the two types of airframe were closely comparable, but because the Comet 3 was able to fly 57% more miles with about the same payload, the maintenance costs were less than two-thirds of the piston-engined aircraft for a given ton-mile of payload. Although fuel consumption for the jet was nearly three times the piston-engined aircraft, the cost of the jet fuel was only two-thirds of petrol and when combined with the higher speed giving greater productivity, the overall fuel costs were

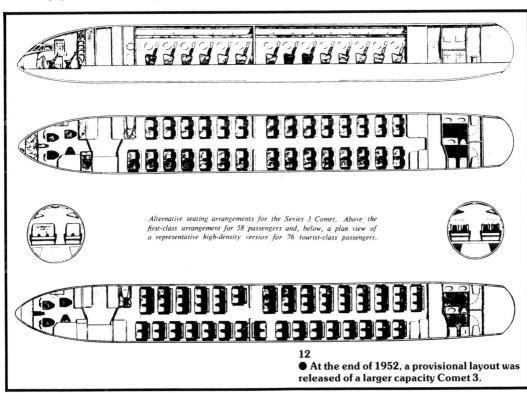

Alternative seating arrangements for the Series 3 Comet. Above, the first-class arrangement for 58 passengers and, below, a plan view of a representative high-density version for 76 tourist-class passengers.

12
● **At the end of 1952, a provisional layout was released of a larger capacity Comet 3.**

49

almost identical. As a result, the higher speed advantage and passenger appeal of the Comet did not result in any increase in costs. Above all, the Comet arrived at destinations well ahead of the competition and where the traveller required shorter journey times, the Comet provided the answer.

Meanwhile, the development programme with the Comet 2 was progressing smoothly. The prototype clearly demonstrated its higher speed with the Rolls-Royce Avon engines when it flew to Africa on its tropical trials. On the outbound journey heading for Khartoum and Entebbe, on 5 May 1953, the Hatfield to Cairo leg was flown at an average speed of 476mph, improving on the official record gained by a Comet 1 by 30min. On the return on 20 May, the official time was reduced by 16min despite strong headwinds. The pilots for these trials were John Cunningham and his deputy, Peter Bugge.

On 27 August 1953, John Cunningham took G-AMXA, the first of 12 Comet 2s for BOAC, on its maiden flight from Hatfield. The development aircraft, G-ALYT, was then made available to BOAC to commence a series of route-proving flights, The first of these arrived at Rio de Janeiro from London on 14 September. The 5,850-mile flight via Lisbon, Dakar and Recife took an elapsed time of 21hr 6min. Both the outbound and return flights flown by BOAC Capt A. P. W. Cane and A. M. Majendie were submitted for recognition as official records, the operation paving the way for the extension of BOAC schedules to South America in 1954.

On 7 August 1953, de Havilland was able to announce another sales success for the Comet 2. With all three Comet 1As delivered to Air France, an order was placed for three Comet 2s for delivery early in 1955. The fuselage was stretched by about 3ft over the earlier aircraft, but the same number of passengers – 44 – would be carried as in the Series 1As with adjustable seats throughout to give greater comfort. The capacity payload of 13,500lb could be carried on stage lengths exceeding 2,000 miles, at an all-up weight of 120,000lb.

On Wednesday 26 August 1953, Air France became the third airline to introduce jet operations when Comet 1A, F-BGNY, left Le Bourget for Beirut via Rome. This was initially a once-a-week service taking 6hr 45min, 3hr 25min faster than previous schedules. On the previous day, the 34th anniversary of the first London to Paris scheduled service, an Air France Comet 1A set up a new Paris to London record by flying the 215 miles in 51min; the AT&T DH4A had taken 2hr 30min in 1919.

The second Comet 2, G-AMXB, joined the development programme with its first flight on 3 November 1953, by which time Comets had flown a total of 30,000hr and were covering 177,000 miles each week. This was equivalent to seven times round the world. With Comet 2s on order for eight airlines, and plans being made for the start of the Comet 3s, production capacity was further increased by allocating additional space in the vast Chester factory, as well as Short Brothers, both of which would be producing Comets during 1954.

Below:
The first Comet 1A for the RCAF, VC5301, made its maiden flight from Hatfield on 21 February 1953.

Right:
RCAF Comet 1A, VC5301, was the first jet transport to cross the North Atlantic when it was delivered to No 412 Squadron at Ottawa on 29 May 1953.

Below right:
The RCAF used the two Comet 1As for VIP transport and also to simulate high-speed jet bomber penetration to test the country's defences.
De Havilland Canada

On 31 October 1953, BOAC completed the first 18 months of Comet jet operations, carrying 155.5 million passenger miles profitably in 21,000 flying hours. Delivery of the first of the Comet 2s for the South American and Australian routes was imminent when BOAC placed an order for five of the larger Comet 3s for the North Atlantic express routes, bringing its total Comet fleet to 25 aircraft, with more on option.

One interesting incident with a BOAC Comet 1 was the unplanned landing at Juhu Aerodrome, Bombay on 16 July 1953. Juhu was the old Bombay flying field with the longest runway of 1,250yd and a difficult approach over houses at the eastern end. Landing from the west was over an unobstructed bathing beach, but on the day the Comet landed, there was a strong westerly wind right down the runway. The aircraft touched down some 500yd from the threshold with a tailwind.

After touchdown, the port bogie left the side of the runway, helping to slow the aircraft and then the aircraft swung sharply to the right, sliding sideways down the runway. The undercarriage stood the strain and the Comet came to rest sideways-on, and close to the boundary fence with nothing worse than burst tyres. No one was hurt. If the aircraft had been able to approach into wind, and touch close to the threshold, it would have stopped easily, instead of having in effect only 750yd. On 24 July, the lightly loaded Comet took off in less than 650yd and was up to 500ft by the time it crossed the boundary.

Following the results of the early flight-testing of the Comet 2, an outline of capabilities and performance was published in early 1954. The aircraft benefited from the lessons learned in nearly two years of commercial operations, as well as the exhaustive testing.

The Comet 2 was a natural development of the Comet 1, taking advantage of the more powerful and economic Rolls-Royce Avon engine, giving an increased all-up weight, larger cabin and greater fuel capacity. By using the sixth Comet 1 airframe G-ALYT as a development vehicle, much experience was gained to the benefit of production aircraft.

One of the modifications incorporated was an improved wing section giving a better take-off performance, improved slow flying characteristics, reduced landing speed, and made it impossible to stall the wing during the take-off run. This latter feature avoided the repetition of the Rome and Karachi accidents.

The Avon as orginally offered developed 6,500lb of thrust, but the development programme had allowed an increase to 7,150lb thrust for service entry. Not only did this improve take-off performance, but the overhaul life was expected to soon reach 1,000hr, once established in regular commercial service. The Comet 2, therefore, had 15,000lb increase in all-up weight over the Comet 1 and able to carry a payload of 13,450lb. The range was adequate for all but the longest trunk routes and the cruising speed was between 480 and 500mph. A typical long-range operation was the 2,116 miles from Caracas to New York in a time of 5hr 19min, carrying the capacity payload. The Comet 2 could also operate profitably the San Francisco to Honolulu stage, a distance of 2,414 miles. Take-off distance was not a problem, but to carry sufficient fuel the payload needed to be reduced to 10,970lb. However, this represented a full load of 44 passengers, their baggage plus 1,080lb of freight.

On 16 November 1953, CPA announced its order for three Comet 2s to be operated on the previously planned Vancouver to Sydney service,

Above:
Comet 2, G-AMXA, was the first of 12 on order for BOAC and made its maiden flight from Hatfield on 27 August 1953.

Above right:
The first Air France Comet 1A, F-BGNX, was delivered to the airline on 12 June 1953.

Right:
Air France Comet 1A, F-BGNY, inaugurated jet operations for the airline on 26 August 1953 with a flight from Paris to Beirut.

which was less suited to the Comet 1A. The 7,500 miles were to be flown with stops at Auckland, Fiji, Canton Island and San Francisco.

Then news came in of the loss of another BOAC Comet 1 in mysterious circumstances. The first production aircraft, G-ALYP, came down in the sea off Elba after take-off from Rome on Sunday 10 January 1954. The aircraft was en route from Singapore to London, and all 29 passengers and six crew were killed. On the following day BOAC, in consultation with de Havilland, temporarily suspended Comet operations to allow detailed checks of the aircraft. Some 60 precautionary modifications were made to the remaining aircraft in the fleet, covering all the suspected causes of the disaster, before the Minister of Transport and Civil Aviation Authority permitted services to be resumed on 23 March.

Meanwhile Comet 2 development continued, with the first production aircraft, G-AMXA, participating in tropical trials at Khartoum and Johannesburg from 22 January to 6 February 1954. The aircraft captained by John Cunningham gained the London to Khartoum record at 481mph in an

elapsed time of 6hr 24min 19sec over a distance of 3,080 miles. The results of the tests not only confirmed predictions, but appeared significantly better than expected. The Comet had left Hatfield at its full all-up weight of 120,000lb, including a full load of fuel of 6,920gal, and a payload of 10,500lb, representing 44 passengers and their baggage. On landing at Khartoum, the base for the high ambient temperature trials, the Comet had sufficient fuel for a 400-mile diversion with a 30min hold for landing. The hot and high trials at Jan Smuts Airport, near Johannesburg, were from an elevation of 5,559ft above sea level, the aircraft performing faultlessly throughout.

Air France confirmed its support for the Comet by adding three more Comet 2s to its fleet, signing the new contract on 31 December 1953. This brought the airline's total commitment to three Comet 1As

already delivered, and six Comet 2s. The Comet 1As were serving Algiers, Casablanca, Beirut and Cairo from Paris, the Comet 2 allowing a further extension of the jet airliner network. BOAC also confirmed its selection of the Comet 3 by signing the contract for five aircraft on 1 February 1954.

The Comet, therefore, was showing every sign of becoming a world-beater, gaining universal acceptance with the airlines and their passengers, who provided consistently high load factors. The Comet was years ahead of the competition pioneering jet transportation, high above the weather and achieving journey times half that expected with piston-engined aircraft. The higher speed gave greater utilisation, helping to bring down the costs of air travel to the public.

The BOAC Comet 1, G-ALYY, was lost off Stromboli on 8 April 1954.

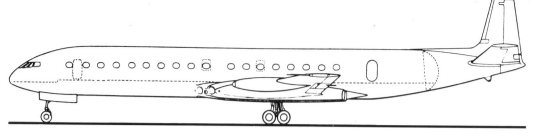

The Comet Investigation

The accident to BOAC Comet 1, 'Yoke-Yoke', on charter to SAA with the loss of all on board, resulted in an immediate grounding of all passenger-carrying Comets and withdrawal of the Certificate of Airworthiness (C of A) on 12 April, pending a full investigation into the cause. G-ALYY had fallen in a deep part of the Mediterranean Sea near Naples, and the majority of the wreckage was beyond recovery. However, work had already commenced by the Royal Navy on the recovery of the wreckage of 'Yoke-Peter' from the sea bed near Elba.

The aircraft lay at depths of between 450 and 600ft of water, and due to the technology available at the time, divers and equipment were only able to go down 200ft. The problem was also to locate the position of the wreckage, which had not been fixed when two Elba fishermen who had seen the aircraft fall, picked up some of the bodies. By pure chance, photographs had been taken of the rescue craft from an aircraft flying overhead, and the position of a part of the coastline of Elba helped to place the main area of the widely scattered wreckage.

The Malta-based salvage vessel, *Sea Salvor*, was taken to the scene and pioneered the use of television to detect possible components. Despite very bad weather and many frustrating delays, *Sea Salvor* located the first major piece of wreckage on 10 February, a month after the loss of the aircraft. The first piece raised was the rear cabin including pressure dome and passenger seats, and eventually about 75% of the aircraft was recovered including the cockpit and the centre section of the cabin and wings, containing all four Ghost engines. No flight data or cockpit voice recorders were carried at this time.

All the recovered parts were taken to RAE Farnborough for the most detailed and searching aircraft investigation ever undertaken, led by Sir

Arnold Hall. A special rig was made to allow the remains of the aircraft to be reassembled to determine how it had broken up, and where the weak link was located.

In parallel to this reconstruction, a fully instrumented Comet 1A, G-ANAV, was test-flown from the RAE to check against the possibility of uncontrolled flutter of a part of the structure causing a catastrophic failure. This aircraft was flown from Heathrow to Farnborough on 24 May 1954 to be adapted with extensive strain gauges and instrumentation and was flown without pressurisation. Also Comet 1, G-ALYU, was installed in a water tank at Farnborough where it was subjected to dynamic pressure testing until failure of the cabin.

With all production of the Comet 2 and 3 stopped and only limited test flying continuing on both types, it was urgent to determine the cause of the accidents and establish a new safety standard to avoid further recurrence. Obviously such a hold-up in flying and production was not only expensive to de Havilland and its customers, but also allowed the competition time to catch up the lead gained by the Comet.

Following the completion of the investigation, a Court of Inquiry was convened in London from 19 October until 24 November 1954. The resultant report was issued on 12 February 1955.

The early part of the report dealt with the design philosophy of the Comet based on current practice at that time. In preparing the Comet cabin to withstand the pressures expected at the high altitudes, de Havilland adopted a multiple of the working pressure — P — which was in excess of any international requirements. Under the British Civil Airworthiness Requirements (BCAR) a proof pressure of 1.5P was called for under which the cabin must not suffer any permanent deformation. The design pressure, 2P, was close to the ultimate strength of the material, but de Havilland designed to 2.5P and tested representative sections to 2P. By completing these rigorous tests satisfactorily, de Havilland, backed by expert opinion and the airworthiness authorities, felt that it had protected against fatigue cracking and possible failure of any of the windows, doors or hatches. In fact the whole aircraft structure was designed in excess of the current requirements, and then proven by exhaustive testing.

In about the middle of 1952 there became an awareness through new knowledge gained, that further work should be undertaken on design and test of a pressure cabin, with particular reference to the non-representative static testing of samples. It was being suggested that cabins should be subjected to a static test to 2P, a proof test to 1.5P and also 15,000 test applications of 1.25P. Static testing could not possibly reproduce fatigue resistance qualities, which would be achieved with dynamic testing.

Comet 2, G-AMXD, was flown on tropical trials at Khartoum and Entebbe in early October 1954. *Flight*

As a result of these developments, de Havilland reconsidered the Comet cabin structure in July 1953. Up to that time, no Comet had exceeded 2,500hr flying, equivalent to about 800 pressurised flights. Therefore, to determine a safe working life of the cabin, repeated loading tests were carried out on one of the earlier specimens of the forward cabin, applying the working pressure P about 16,000 times. The tests continued on this specimen, which had originally had some 30 earlier applications of between P and 2P, until the cabin failed at the corner of a window due to fatigue caused by a small defect in the skin. However, the number of pressurisations was so large that it was felt that the safety of the Comet's cabin was established with an ample margin.

Following the failure of the cabin in the test section, de Havilland did design the Comet 3 with oval windows, to reduce the higher stress points experienced in the corners of square or rectangular cut-outs.

Meanwhile, Comet 1, G-ALYV, had been lost on 2 May 1953 in an exceptionally violent storm, causing structural failure of the airframe. Fatigue failure of the cabin was not suspected, and the subsequent inquiry saw no reason to change the findings of the earlier accident.

Immediately following the loss of G-ALYP, passenger services were suspended to carry out detailed examinations of the aircraft in collaboration with BOAC, de Havilland Aircraft and the engine companies, the Air Registration Board (ARB) and the Accidents Branch of the Ministry of Transport and Civil Aviation. A committee was formed under the chairmanship of Mr Charles Abell, Deputy Operations Director (Engineering) of BOAC to consider the likely causes and preventative measures.

The main possible causes considered were as follows: flutter of control surfaces, requiring a thorough inspection of the control systems; primary structural failure, due to violent gusts, requiring a study of the airframe to determine any weaknesses; flying control malfunction causing catastrophic loss of control, requiring a study of the hydraulic power units; fatigue of the structure, in particular the wing; explosive decompression of the cabin; although the primary structure was not suspect, studies were made of the window panels where defects may not have been revealed by the manufacturer's testing; and finally the engine installation, where fire risk was studied and any areas of doubt were removed by modification.

The conclusions of the committee was that probably fire was the cause of the aircraft loss and a large number of precautionary modifications were made to cover all the areas of study. As a result approval was given for services to recommence on 23 March 1954.

The dramatic similarity of the sudden loss of G-ALYY on 8 April 1954, when on charter to SAA, resulted in a further grounding of the entire airline fleet of Comets and the subsequent withdrawal of the C of A. Both aircraft were at approximately the same height and about the same time outbound from Rome, but in different directions.

The RAE, under the direction of Sir Arnold Hall, were tasked to undertake a thorough investigation, not only in the interest of the Comet, but obviously in the interests of civil aviation throughout the world. The RAE concentrated its investigations on the structural integrity of the Comet, particularly the cabin and the tail, and considered in greater detail the possible sources of explosion and loss of control. It was also decided that flight testing would

be necessary to investigate flutter of the control surfaces, the task undertaken by G-ANAV.

Meanwhile, the recovery of the wreckage of G-ALYP was going better than expected with the wing centre section received on 5 April, followed by the forward cabin 10 days later. The engines had been shipped to de Havilland Engine Company for assessment. At this stage failure of the pressure cabin was suspected as the prime cause, due to the similarity of the accidents and particularly as most other causes had been ruled out by the incorporation of modifications.

As a result, G-ALYU was immersed in a water tank at Farnborough and repeated loading tests started in June to simulate the conditions of a series of pressurised flights. The cabin and wings were subjected to loadings as nearly representative as possible of operational conditions between take-off and landing. The normal pressure loads P were administered, and every 1,000 'flights' a proof test of 1.5P equal to 11.5lb/sq in was used.

'Yoke-Uncle' had made 1,230 pressure flights before the test, and after the equivalent of a further 1,830 simulated flights, making a total of 3,060, the cabin structure failed at the corner of one of the cabin windows, due to fatigue.

From this point the dominant feature of the investigation was centred upon structural failure of the cabin, although other possibilities were still being considered. The cabin of G-ALYU was repaired by de Havilland and the tests continued with strain gauges fixed to the suspect areas of the skin, where the stresses were found to be much in excess of those anticipated. At a pressure differential in the cabin of 8.25lb/sq in, the highest stress at the corner of the windows was in excess of 40,000lb/sq in. However, with the variation in the structures caused by material specifications and methods of manufacture, the test on one specimen was not a conclusive measurement for the life of similar airframes. For example, the cabin of 'Yoke-Peter' failed after 1,290 pressurised flights, and 'Yoke-Yoke' only completed 900 flights.

As a result of the continuing salvage attempts on 'Yoke-Peter', a piece of cabin skin was identified as having come from the centre of the top cabin, approximately over the wing front spar. It contained the cutouts for the ADF (Automatic Direction Finding) aerials. At the same time part of the port aileron and part of the port boundary layer fence fitted on the leading edge near the wingtip was received by the RAE.

These two areas of the airframe provided conclusive evidence confirming the bursting of the cabin. There were marks on the wing components made by pieces of the cabin. Taken together with the paint marks in the leading edge of the wing centre section, just inboard from where the outer wing failed, identified as being caused by the cabin skin containing the first window with escape hatch,

it was established that the cabin burst catastrophically around the area of the wing front spar during normal flight.

By examination of the piece containing the ADF aerial and adjacent pieces, it was established that the fracture commenced along the top centre of the cabin passing through corners of the ADF aerial cutout windows. It was most likely to have started near the starboard aft corner of the rear ADF window where fatigue existed, at the edge of a countersunk hole, through which a bolt passed.

All four Ghost engines were checked and found to have been operating normally up to the time of

Below:

For a while, de Havilland marketed the Comet 2 and Comet 3 as a complementary pair. However, delays during the accident investigation outdated the concept.

Bottom:

Comet 1, G-ALYX, was used for prolonged engine runs at Hatfield in 1954 to investigate the effects of jet exhaust noise damage to the fuselage structure.

the accident, with no sign of pre-crash failure or excessive internal heating. No turbine blades had been lost, all the engine damage having been caused by the sudden violent break-up of the aircraft.

The report did mention the experience by BOAC of the Comets in service having a small amount of damage due to buffeting by the efflux from the jet engines. The damage was both fore and aft of the rear cabin pressure dome. As soon as the damage was noted, all aircraft were inspected and repaired where necessary. The situation was observed

continuously on the existing Comets, and later aircraft had the jet-pipes angled out slightly to take the damaging exhaust well clear of the skin.

The original design philosophy of the Comet by de Havilland was studied by the inquiry. The company did not make detailed calculations of the stress at the corners of the cabin windows, preferring to calculate stresses in general areas around the windows and then proving the design integrity by static testing of selected cabin samples. Since the general level of stress in the selected areas was under half the ultimate strength of the material, if there was no failure in static test to twice the pressure differential, then there should be sufficient reserve available. The tests of three square panels containing a window confirmed these predictions.

Unfortunately these tests were not on a representative section of the cabin, as at no stage was a full cabin tested, and all sections were quite naturally supported by steel pressure bulkheads. With the agreement of the ARB, de Havilland believed the pressure cabins to have a safe life of at least 10 years.

Below:
Following the return of the Air France Comet 1As, F-BGNY was temporarily re-registered G-AOJU. It later became XM829 at Boscombe Down as a flying laboratory.

Bottom:
Comet 1A, XM829, was retired to the Stansted Fire School after its service at Boscombe Down. *Author*

When de Havilland began investigating fatigue testing of the cabin sections from mid-1952 to the end of 1953, the front section of the test cabin survived 16,000 simulated pressurised flights, taking the expected safe life to beyond 10 years. The RAE measured stresses at the window corners using strain gauges which led to an estimated stress of 43,000lb/sq in when a normal pressure differential of 8.25lb/sq in was applied. This measurement was regarded as unreliable by de Havilland as it would have meant stresses of 86,000lb/sq in when the working pressure was doubled on test, which was some 30% above the ultimate strength of the material. However, the ductility of the metal had not been considered, which relieved stress concentration.

Although the stress levels around the windows could not be calculated with any precision, due to the influence of other parts of the structure, the higher than expected values were confirmed by the failure of 'Yoke-Uncle'. The stresses were probably in excess of 40,000lb/sq in under normal pressure differential. Whereas the sharp differences of opinion existed between de Havilland and the RAE at the start of the inquiry, as time progressed a greater mutual understanding developed.

The probable explanation for the original de Havilland test specimen having a much longer life than 'Yoke-Uncle' at the RAE could well have been due to its earlier tests to a differential pressure of 16.5lb/sq in, which could prolong the life of the specimen.

Another area of criticism of de Havilland was its method for dealing with cracks in the skin detected or caused during manufacture. It was generally accepted practice that for cracks in areas of low stress, they could be stopped by drilling a small hole through the skin at the end of the crack. Cracks in higher stress areas could be repaired, and if found to continue would be investigated.

For the future design of pressure cabins following the accidents, it was necessary to achieve a safe life with the lightest possible structure. More study in design and by experiment was necessary, before definite standards could be set. Testing would therefore have to be revised to include the complete cabin, to confirm the results of more detailed calculations. The tests were expected to include two complete cabins, one for the ultimate static proof test and the other for a series of dynamic tests to determine fatigue properties.

With all the knowledge gained from the inquiry it

Top:
The two RCAF Comet 1As returned to de Havilland to have their cabins strengthened and the fitting of oval windows.

Above:
In October 1964, the first RCAF Comet was dismantled after retirement, but the second aircraft survived until the late 1960s in the USA.

was expected that de Havilland would redesign the Comet and submit the new aircraft to the ARB for approval. A recommendation was also made, following the loss of G-ALYV near Calcutta, that the pilot should have a positive feel built into the power control system to represent flight loads. This would avoid the pilot over-controlling and over-stressing the aircraft in manoeuvres.

The accident to G-ALYP was not due to the wrongful act or default or to the negligence of any party, or of any person in the employment of any party. De Havilland was, therefore, in no way held to blame for the loss of the aircraft, since it was working to approved practices based on the knowledge available. Due to the lack of recovered wreckage from G-ALYY off Naples it was assumed, that with many similarities, the cause must have

been the same. No blame was attached to anyone in connection with the resumption to services after G-ALYP was lost, as all known possible precautions had been taken by the manufacturer and the airline, with the full approval of the airworthiness authorities.

Meanwhile, although Comet production had been halted during the investigation and all commercial services stopped, development testing had continued on the Comet 2 and larger Comet 3.

The Comet 3 was rolled out of the Experimental hangar at Hatfield on 4 May 1954, ready to commence engine runs. The new aircraft was 18ft longer than the Comet 1 and the all-up weight of 150,000lb would be propelled by four 10,000lb thrust Avon engines. The Comet 2 and Comet 3 were offered as partners in airline operations worldwide. At the same time as the prototype G-ANLO was being readied for engine tests, the first production fuselage was pressure proof-tested. This fuselage was later to be used as a structural test specimen, eventually to destruction.

The Comet made its first flight from Hatfield on 19 July 1954, under the command of John Cunningham. The flight was made after the customary high-speed taxi runs and a couple of

short hops. It took off at 17.30hrs and landed 1hr 25min later, having performed satisfactorily. It was then able to accumulate sufficient test hours to participate in the SBAC display at Farnborough in September, which it shared with a production Comet 2. By mid-November, the new Comet had made some 50 flights.

All the oval passenger windows were forward of the jet pipe exhausts, which were swept away from the cabin to reduce noise and avoid damage. The air intakes for the new Avon engines were about twice the area of the Comet 1, and the wing leading edge-mounted pinion tanks held 856gal of the total of 8,374gal of fuel.

Development flying also continued on the Comet 2. With the delay caused by the investigation, more powerful Rolls-Royce Avon engines were fitted to G-AMXD, each developing a thrust of 7,300lb. As a result of these more powerful engines, a supplementary series of tropical trials was held in Africa from 30 September until 7 October. Khartoum was used for hot weather take-off trials and Entebbe, situated at 3,760ft, for hot and high take-off trials. These trials were part of obtaining a new C of A for the Comet 2, required for the international passenger operations with the RAF, but at this stage, G-AMXD did not have the strengthened cabin, which was later modified when the RA29 Avon engines were fitted. The aircraft was operated at its maximum all-up weight of 120,000lb, the full capacity payload of 13,000lb being largely represented by ballast.

However, while this development work continued, there was no production of new aircraft, and in the event no Comets emerged from the Shorts factory in Belfast. All the sales prospects quickly

Above:
The Comet 2 flightdeck differed little from the Comet 1.

Left:
A water tank was built at Hatfield to test the Comet 2 airframe, with sufficient length to be able to accommodate the larger Comet 4.

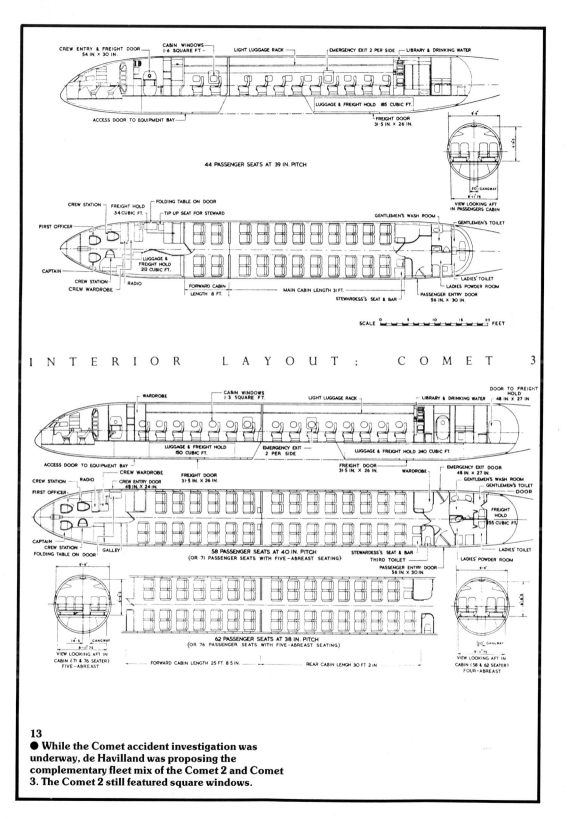

CREW ENTRY & FREIGHT DOOR
54 IN. X 30 IN.

CABIN WINDOWS
1·6 SQUARE FT.

LIGHT LUGGAGE RACK

EMERGENCY EXIT 2 PER SIDE

LIBRARY & DRINKING WATER

ACCESS DOOR TO EQUIPMENT BAY

LUGGAGE & FREIGHT HOLD 185 CUBIC FT.

FREIGHT DOOR
31·5 IN. X 26 IN.

44 PASSENGER SEATS AT 39 IN. PITCH

VIEW LOOKING AFT
IN PASSENGERS CABIN

20° GANGWAY

CREW STATION

FREIGHT HOLD
34 CUBIC FT.

FOLDING TABLE ON DOOR

TIP UP SEAT FOR STEWARD

GENTLEMEN'S WASH ROOM

FIRST OFFICER

GENTLEMEN'S TOILET

LUGGAGE &
FREIGHT HOLD
212 CUBIC FT.

CAPTAIN

LADIES' TOILET

CREW STATION
CREW WARDROBE

RADIO

FORWARD CABIN
LENGTH 8 FT.

MAIN CABIN LENGTH 31 FT.

STEWARDESS'S SEAT & BAR

LADIES POWDER ROOM

PASSENGER ENTRY DOOR
56 IN. X 30 IN.

SCALE 0 5 10 15 20 FEET

I N T E R I O R   L A Y O U T :   C O M E T   3

WARDROBE

CABIN WINDOWS
1·3 SQUARE FT.

LIGHT LUGGAGE RACK

LIBRARY & DRINKING WATER

DOOR TO FREIGHT
HOLD
48 IN. X 27 IN

LUGGAGE & FREIGHT HOLD
150 CUBIC FT.

EMERGENCY EXIT
2 PER SIDE

LUGGAGE & FREIGHT HOLD 240 CUBIC FT.

ACCESS DOOR TO EQUIPMENT BAY

CREW WARDROBE

FREIGHT DOOR
31·5 IN. X 26 IN.

FREIGHT DOOR
31·5 IN. X 26 IN.

WARDROBE

EMERGENCY EXIT DOOR
48 IN. X 27 IN.

CREW STATION

RADIO

CREW ENTRY DOOR
48 IN. X 24 IN.

GENTLEMEN'S WASH ROOM

GENTLEMEN'S TOILET

FIRST OFFICER

DOOR

FREIGHT
HOLD
355 CUBIC FT.

CAPTAIN

CREW STATION
FOLDING TABLE ON DOOR

GALLEY

58 PASSENGER SEATS AT 40 IN. PITCH
(OR 71 PASSENGER SEATS WITH FIVE-ABREAST SEATING)

STEWARDESS'S SEAT & BAR
THIRD TOILET

PASSENGER ENTRY DOOR
56 IN. X 30 IN.

LADIES' TOILET

LADIES' POWDER ROOM

9'-9"

20° GANGWAY

62 PASSENGER SEATS AT 38 IN. PITCH
(OR 76 PASSENGER SEATS WITH FIVE-ABREAST SEATING)

14·5 GANGWAY
8-11·75

VIEW LOOKING AFT IN
CABIN (71 & 76 SEATER)
FIVE-ABREAST

FORWARD CABIN LENGTH 25 FT. 8·5 IN.

REAR CABIN LENGH 30 FT. 2 IN.

8-11·75

VIEW LOOKING AFT IN
CABIN (58 & 62 SEATER)
FOUR-ABREAST

13

● While the Comet accident investigation was
underway, de Havilland was proposing the
complementary fleet mix of the Comet 2 and Comet
3. The Comet 2 still featured square windows.

evaporated when neither firm delivery dates, prices nor specifications could be guaranteed. From being world leader in the production of jet airliners, the harsh learning curve had returned to zero.

Although no Comet 2s had been delivered, there were scattered around the world some grounded Comet 1 and 1As which were expensive liabilities to their once proud owners. The two prototypes had finished their useful life, the first one being scrapped in 1953 after structural testing, while the second prototype was used to test the pinion tank installation for the Comet 3 before it was finally dismantled in 1957. BOAC still had six aircraft, but these were all allocated to various aspects of the investigation. G-ALYR had been damaged when it skidded off the runway at Calcutta, and was returned to Britain for repairs, but in the event used for structural testing at Farnborough. G-ALYS was used for systems and buffet investigations at the RAE and dismantled in 1955. As already recorded G-ALYU was the main water tank test specimen at Farnborough and G-ALYW went to the RAE for tests in 1955 before being dismantled and the fuselage survives as an RAF recruiting Nimrod simulator. G-ALYX was used for integral tank tests at Hatfield and then became a nuisance to the neighbours when it was allocated to extensive engine running tests, to check for structural damage to the fuselage caused by engine exhaust. It was scrapped in 1955. The final BOAC aircraft, Comet 1A, G-ANAV, was scrapped at Farnborough on completion of its test flying programme, and the nose was donated as an exhibit to the London Science Museum.

Of the three UAT Comet 1As, F-BGSC had already been damaged beyond repair at Dakar in June 1953, and the other two sat at Le Bourget after the grounding on 12 April 1954, until they were eventually scrapped.

All three of the Air France Comet 1As were bought by the British Ministry of Supply and returned to Britain. F-BGNX was re-registered G-AOJT for its flight to the RAE on 27 June 1956,

Above:
Two Comet 2s, G-AMXD and G-AMXK, were converted with Avon RA29 engines in the outboard position for Comet 4 engine development. G-AMXK was delivered to BOAC on 26 August 1957 for route-proving trials.

Above right:
Comet 2E, G-AMXD, was delivered to Farnborough as XN453 to be used as a flying laboratory. *Author*

Right:
Comet 2E, G-AMXK, was used by Smiths Industries for autopilot development, after service with BOAC. *Author*

Below right:
Comet 2E, G-AMXK, was delivered to RAE Bedford as XV144 for use by the Blind Landing Experimental Unit (BLEU). *Author*

where it was dismantled and the fuselage cocooned for possible use as a structural test specimen. However, this did not come to pass and the familiar grey cigar shape became part of the Farnborough scenery for many years until finally acquired on 20 March 1985 by the Mosquito Aircraft Museum for preservation and eventual restoration. This fuselage still has the square windows, but is missing all of the original internal equipment. The other two Air France aircraft, 'NY and 'NZ, became respectively G-AOJU and G-APAS, then after modifications including new cabin skins with oval windows as Mk 1XBs, they undertook programmes of research flying as XM829 and XM823. XM829 was flown from Boscombe Down on navigation systems trials, until it was delivered to the Fire School at Stansted on 20 February 1964. It finally succumbed to the torches in the autumn of 1970. XM823 was used by de Havilland Propellers for missile trials, appearing in some bizarre colour schemes. One was overall silver with a Day-Glo band along the cheat line, but the most wayout was matt black overall with a Day-Glo patch over the

centre fuselage. The aircraft was finally painted in the standard RAF transport livery and as such was saved from scrap and flown to Shawbury on 8 April 1968, where it was in open storage for the RAF Museum. Its final move was by road 10 years later to the RAF Museum reserve collection at Cosford where it was painted to represent a BOAC aircraft.

Both the RCAF Comets were flown to Chester where they were modified with new cabin skins and oval windows, returning to service with No 412

Squadron in 1957. Both were retired in 1964 and offered for sale, but no conclusive purchase came up and the two aircraft quietly vanished from the scene after a number of changes of ownership.

A total of 14 Comet 2s were eventually completed at Hatfield and one from Chester, the majority being operated by the RAF. Two, G-AMXD and G-AMXK, were originally allocated to engine development work, with the two outboard earlier Avon engines replaced by the more powerful Rolls-Royce RA29 Avon destined for the ultimate Comet 4, then under development. Both aircraft with strengthened cabins and oval windows were operated by BOAC on typical routes to gain experience with the engines and to provide endurance testing.

G-AMXD then was allocated to RAE Farn-borough as XN453 for long-range radio aid development. It was finally retired to RAE Bedford in February 1973. After service with BOAC, G-AMXK returned to Hatfield to be operated by Smith's Instruments for the early development of their automatic landing system. It was used on autoflare work until the end of 1962 and was then fitted with the SEP 5, autoland and flight system for the Short Belfast in mid-1963. It became XV144 in March 1966 for delivery to the Blind Landing Experimental Unit (BLEU) at RAE Bedford on 18 November 1966. It was retired on 18 May 1971 to Farnborough where it provided a source of spares until it was finally scrapped in 1976.

The remaining 13 Comet 2s were modified for use by the RAF, three on signals duties and the other 10 for transport duties with No 216 Squadron. More of these operations will be dealt with in greater detail in a later chapter.

The only other early Comet whose fate has not been dealt with is the prototype Mk 2, G-ALYT. This aircraft continued as an unpressurised engine test bed, fitted with the Avon 502s as used in the Comet 3, and later a single RA29. This faithful old workhorse was finally flown into the short grass airfield at RAF Halton by John Cunningham on 15 June 1959, where it became a ground instruction airframe until finally scrapped in September 1967.

Left:
The original Comet 2 prototype, G-ALYT, was used for Avon engine icing trials, with a water spray rig in front of the engine.

Below:
The Comet 2 prototype, G-ALYT, was finally retired to RAF Halton for ground instruction on 15 June 1959, when John Cunningham landed it on the grass airfield.
Author

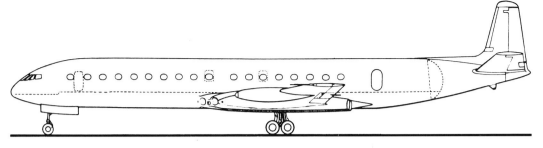

Comet 4 Development

As well as the lessons of investigation itself, the time taken to complete the inquiry had allowed developments to take place which outdated the Comet 3. The pressure cabin had to be built from a thicker gauge less fatigue-resistant aluminium alloy, and production techniques had to be drastically improved in the light of experience. Obviously crack detection had to be more thorough and where countersunk rivets were to be used to give a lower drag, the skin was spin dimpled to retain the strength. For a while the Comet 2 was still on offer, but its economics were less attractive for commercial operations, and it provided a useful vehicle to introduce the RAF to jet transport operations.

On 17 March 1955, de Havilland announced its programme for a new world jet airliner known as the Comet 4, with a launch order from BOAC for 20 aircraft. Amongst the changes were a redesigned fuselage, increased fuel capacity and power from four Rolls-Royce RA29 Avon jet engines giving increased thrust of 500lb, with improved consumption. The range of the new aircraft allowed 58 first

Above:
Following the conclusion of the Comet investigation, BOAC placed an order on 17 March 1955 for 20 of the new Comet 4s.

class passengers to be carried on stage lengths of up to 2,870 miles, allowing London to Johannesburg with two intermediate stops. Other planned routes were to Tokyo and London to New York with a refuelling stop at Gander.

The Comet 4 was evolved from the Comet 3, which it superseded, but the Comet 3 prototype, G-ANLO, continued test flying as an aerodynamic prototype for the new version, since the physical dimensions were identical. When its test flying for the Comet 4 programme was complete, the outer wings were removed and replaced by the smaller wings without pinion tanks to become an aerodynamic test vehicle for the high density Comet 4B for BEA. In this form, it was known as the Comet 3B and made its first flight on 21 August 1958.

On completion of that development programme, the Comet 3B became XP915 and was delivered to the BLEU at RAE Bedford on 21 June 1961 for work on autoland testing. On 19 January 1971, when waiting on the threshold of the runway at Bedford, it was hit by an approaching BEA Trident 3, G-AWZA, which knocked off the fin and wrinkled the fuselage. The Comet was repaired

Above:

The Comet 3 prototype, G-ANLO, was externally identical to the Comet 4, allowing aerodynamic testing to proceed while the new aircraft was under construction. *Charles E. Brown*

using a fin cannibalised from one of the Comet 2s and continued to fly until retirement at the end of 1972. RAE Bedford then used the aircraft for

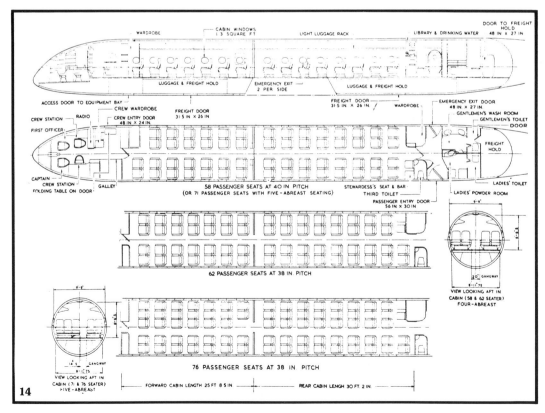

Above:
**Following the completion of Comet 4 development
flying, the extension wings were changed to
represent the Comet 4B wings, and G-ANLO
became the Comet 3B. It first flew in this form on
21 August 1958.** *Charles E. Brown*

non-flying foam arrester trials in 1973, on
completion of which the aircraft was dismantled and
the fuselage used as a Nimrod mock-up at Hawker
Siddeley Aviation (HSA), Woodford.

The Comet 4 was expected to enter service in
1958, the aerodynamically identical Comet 3
providing detailed performance information, as well
as stall development and take-off performance. This
invaluable representative prototype testing reduced
significantly the development flying on the Comet
4, allowing early entry into commercial service. The
new Comet 4 took advantage of all the earlier
airline experience to produce a more reliable
aircraft, and the results of the accident inquiry
ensured structural integrity. By careful attention to
design, stress levels were kept to a minimum in the
fuselage skin joints and around the cutouts, so that
any damage would be fail safe.

Developing 10,500lb of thrust, the RA29 Avon
engines gave a reduction of around 9% in cruising
specific fuel consumption when compared with the
RA26 engines in the Comet 3. The maximum all-up
weight was increased by 2,500lb from the Comet 3,
to a total of 152,500lb. Usable fuel capacity was
also increased to 8,750gal. The capacity payload of
the Comet 4 was expected to be 16,850lb.

The new Avon engines fitted to the Comet 4 gave
it a very lively take-off performance, the runway
length at sea level with a temperature of 30°C
needing 2,380yd at maximum all-up weight. This,
of course, allowed for the failure of one engine at
the critical point of take-off.

Optimum cruising speed corresponded to a Mach
number of 0.74, which was equivalent to 489mph
in standard atmosphere.

The range of cabin accommodation varied from
58 passengers, seated four-abreast at 40in pitch, to
76 passengers, five-abreast at 38in pitch. The
Comet 4 could fly the 3,502 miles from London to
New York in 9hr 30min, with one refuelling stop,
and 5,844 miles from London to Rio with one stop
in just under 14hr. The aircraft was operated by a
crew of four.

14
● **In mid-1955, following the
publication of the Comet
inquiry, de Havilland issued a
preliminary statement on the
new Comet 4.**

Right:
**The Comet 3 eventually joined
the BLEU at RAE Bedford as
XP915 on autoland
development.** *Author*

By late in the summer of 1955, these preliminary performance figures were expected to improve as a result of further flight testing on the Comet 3. The practical stage length at capacity payload had increased by 145 miles to 2,945 miles, by using a higher rate of climb to reduce stage time. The capacity payload with 58 first class passengers was 16,400lb and for the 76-seat tourist class version it was 19,300lb. The improved performance allowed the Comet 4 to fly from London to Johannesburg with only one stop in an elapsed time of 13hr. This is about the same time taken by the SAA Jumbo jets which have to fly around the West African coastline to avoid overflying the countries of Black Africa. The Comet 4 could also fly nonstop from New York to San Francisco with a capacity payload.

The Comet 4 still did not have full nonstop London to New York capability, but de Havilland felt that an aircraft with such a performance would be too large for the average worldwide routes, and therefore too specialised. The Comet however was an ideal size and range for the transcontinental, South Atlantic and Pacific routes.

By the middle of 1955 the major design programme of the Comet 4 was complete and production had commenced ready for deliveries at

the end of 1958. Structural test specimens were built, culminating in a complete airframe, the second built, which was installed in a water tank at Hatfield, and was in fact one of the 20 aircraft ordered by BOAC.

The Comet 3 prototype was fitted with RA29 Avon engines in 1956 allowing some 80% of the C of A flying to be completed before the maiden flight of the Comet 4 scheduled for late 1957, allowing full production to be established at an early stage. As mentioned in the previous chapter, two specially adapted Comet 2Es were used for additional RA29 engine development and endur-

ance testing. By the time the Comet 4 entered service the new Avon engines would have flown some 4,000hr on development. With this and all the other structural and flight testing, the new Comet 4 was the most thoroughly tried and tested airliner in existence.

Some 3,000 separate fatigue tests were conducted on specimen assemblies and the fuselage fatigue life was expected to achieve more than 100,000 pressurisations. A Comet 2 was adapted to the structural standards of the Comet 4 and used for preliminary testing of both the new aircraft, but also to prove the aircraft to enter service with the RAF.

In December 1955, John Cunningham captained the Comet 3 on a round-the-world flight. The object of the exercise was to study the operational performance of the aircraft, flying strictly in accordance with airline procedure on representative stages of a familiar trade route around the world through a variety of climatic conditions. The aircraft flew in the colours of BOAC and Capt Peter Cane, who had headed the Comet 1 fleet for BOAC, shared the flying with John Cunningham and his deputy Peter Bugge. Where BOAC was not directly represented, the aircraft was handled by the resident airline at the port of call, including Qantas, TAA and CPA, gaining additional experience. Full opportunity was taken to demonstrate the aircraft to a number of operators, airworthiness authorities, press and the public. On many of the routes, locally based airline crew participated in the operation of the aircraft.

The departure from a foggy Hatfield was at 10.54hrs GMT on 2 December, heading for Sydney, via Cairo, Bombay, Singapore and Darwin. Because the fog delayed departure planned for 05.00hrs GMT, a night stop was made at Cairo, and arrival at Sydney on the Sunday afternoon after 24hr 24min flying time. After demonstrations in Australia, G-ANLO flew to Auckland, in New Zealand and then across the Pacific via Fiji and Honolulu to Vancouver. The aircraft crossed Canada to Toronto and Montreal before setting out across the North Atlantic, flying directly to London Airport in 6hr 8min, a distance of 3,350 miles arriving on 28 December. The aircraft flew some 30,000 miles round the globe, experiencing the heat of the tropics to minus 15°F in Montreal.

Not only was the Comet 3 highly reliable throughout the entire tour — the only technical fault being the attachment of the No 3 engine jet pipe — but it was found to be a welcome addition to many

Left:
In mid-1957, de Havilland announced the continental Comet 4B, with a lengthened fuselage for up to 100 passengers and shorter span wings for higher speeds at mid-altitudes. *BEA*

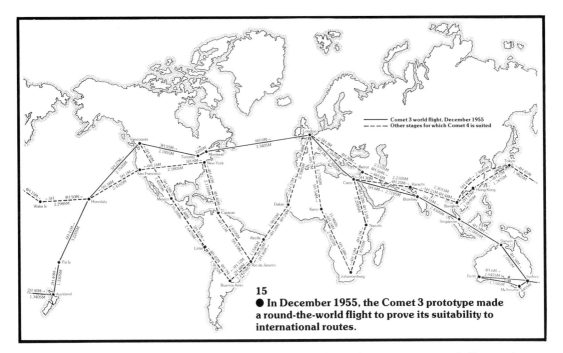

15
● In December 1955, the Comet 3 prototype made a round-the-world flight to prove its suitability to international routes.

airports unfamiliar to jet airliner operations. The low wing-loading made it docile on the approach, the good power-to-weight ratio lifted the Comet away rapidly and it fitted in well with existing runway and take-off patterns. As part of the worldwide marketing programme, some 600 passengers experienced the smoothness of jet operations, despite the rather basic standard of furnishing of the cabin. What was clearly demonstrated was the Comet's capability to achieve worldwide scheduled operations with a high level of reliability and regularity.

Meanwhile a new pressure test-tank had been commissioned at Hatfield to simulate a Comet flight every 4min. The first trial runs started on 26 November 1955 using the strengthened Comet 2 airframe c/n 06036. The fuselage was completely submerged in the tank with the wings protruding out each side through water seals allowing flexing movements of the wings. The tank was large enough to accommodate a complete Comet 4 fuselage, but having the shorter Comet 2

allowed simultaneous testing of Comet 4 production standard major fuselage sections in the separated forward section of the tank. The loads applied to the airframe under test were designed to reproduce all the flight loads which would lead to fatigue in the structure. These loads included simulating a flight with full pressurisation in the fuselage, vertical tail gust loads and vertical wing loads with gust action superimposed on the steady flight loads. The fuselage pressure was increased by pumping in about 100gal of water to achieve a differential of 8.25lb, and hydraulic jacks were used to simulate gusts and flight loads. Safety devices were built into the pressurisation tests to avoid an overload which could extend the life of the test airframe, as was found with the Comet 1. While simulating a typical 3hr sortie on the Comet 2, 24 gusts of 10ft/sec were applied, representing the most critical fatigue case in the Comet structure. The majority of gusts would be in practice at lower altitudes when the cabin would be at a lower pressure differential.

Right:
While waiting on the runway to take-off on 19 January 1971, Comet 3, XP915, was struck by Trident 3, G-AWZA, on crew training. The Comet was repaired and continued to fly until mid-1972. *RAE Bedford*

Right:
In December 1955, John Cunningham and his team took the Comet 3 on a round-the-world flight, calling in at Honolulu.

16
● **The new pressure tank was commissioned at Hatfield in November 1955, the initial test specimen being the Comet 2 and later the Comet 4.**

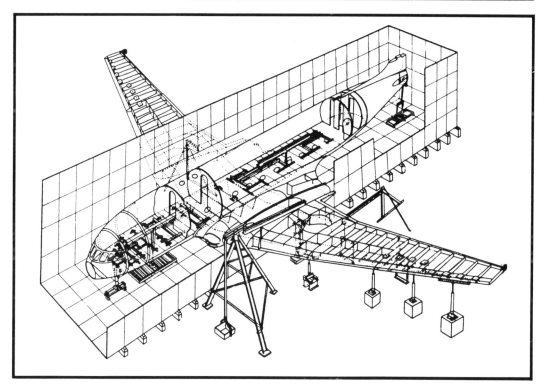

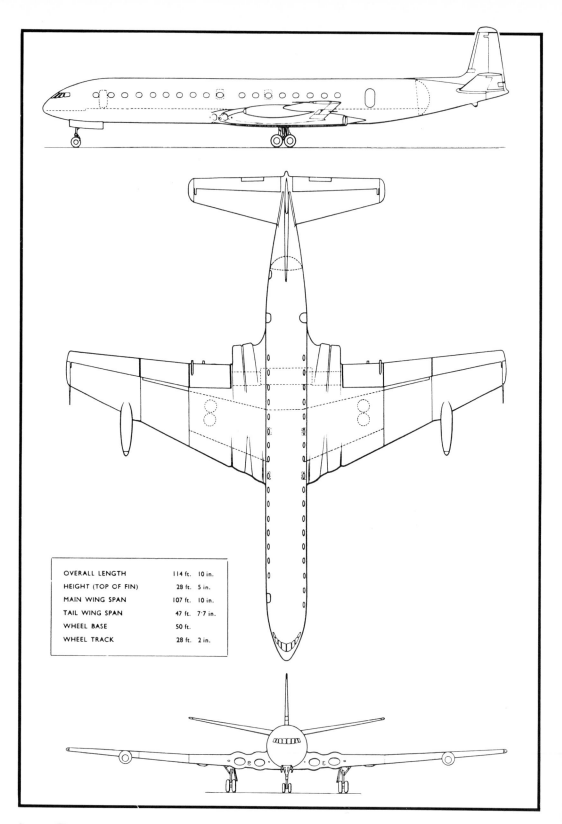

OVERALL LENGTH	114 ft.	10 in.
HEIGHT (TOP OF FIN)	28 ft.	5 in.
MAIN WING SPAN	107 ft.	10 in.
TAIL WING SPAN	47 ft.	7·7 in.
WHEEL BASE	50 ft.	
WHEEL TRACK	28 ft.	2 in.

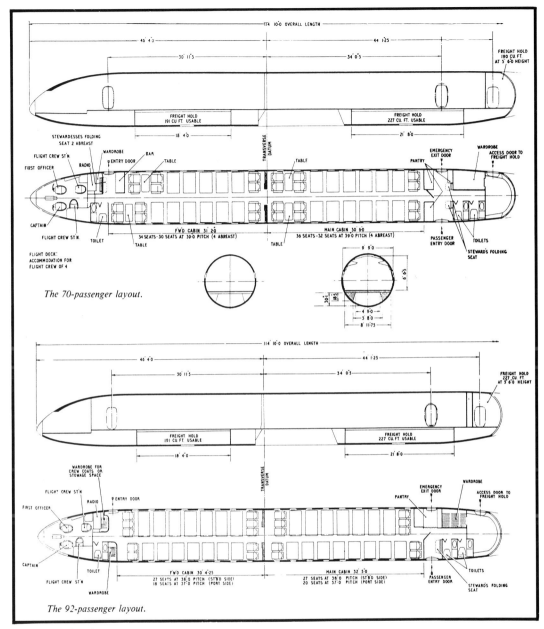

The 70-passenger layout.

The 92-passenger layout.

17 (left and above)
● **The short to medium-haul Comet 4A was announced in the summer of 1956.**

The flight loads were reproduced automatically every 4min by applying steady loads to the wing, lifting it off its undercarriage supports to represent take-off. During the initial climb phase, 10 gusts were simulated on the unpressurised fuselage, followed by four more as the pressure built up. Then with full pressure, four more gusts were loaded, followed by six more as the pressure was reduced in the descent. Finally the flight loads were

removed as the undercarriage took the weight again.

These tests were continued round the clock for under 48hr, simulating 1,500hr flying time. The tank was then emptied for inspection of the airframe, before running for a further 1,500hr. The aim of the test programme was to demonstrate that no fatigue cracks would occur in the structure before a minimum of 60,000 reversals, and that any subsequent cracks would be contained within a further 60,000 reversals. This would give a safe life for the specimen of 180,000hr but, allowing for a scatter factor of six, gave a safe life of 30,000 flying hours.

A 28ft-long representative Comet 4 fuselage section was built with the rear pressure dome and featuring all the normal cutouts in the structure, such as windows, escape hatch, passenger entry and freight doors, luggage bay door, toilet drains and de-icer pipe outlet. A 27ft-long fuselage centre section was tested including flight loads and also a nose section. All these tests were eventually followed by a full representative airframe of the Comet 4.

Not only was the cabin tested but so was the other structure including wing spar booms, lower wing skins and many of the skin joints. This major programme of testing was able to prove without doubt the high structural integrity of the Comet 4.

As a result of operational experience, the many major design improvements on the Comet 4 included increased flap area for greater drag on the approach. Hydraulic and electrical equipment were stowed in completely separate bays and much work had been done to improve the flame-proof qualities of the electrical equipment. Anti-skid brakes were fitted to the undercarriage and reverse thrust was fitted to the outer engines. Improved jet nozzles were fitted to reduce engine noise. The flightdeck was redesigned to accommodate five crew, and the cabin layout could be readily adapted from first class to tourist, removing the original scheme of first class operation only.

In the summer of 1956, de Havilland announced the Comet 4A, a short- to medium-haul version giving competitive economy with high-speed cruise at medium altitudes. The Comet 4 was still offered for the longer stage routes. The Comet 4A was to be lengthened by 40in, allowing up to 95 passengers to be carried in economy class with five-abreast seating. The wingspan was reduced from 115ft to 108ft, enabling high cruising speeds to be obtained at lower altitudes. The maximum zero-fuel weight was increased by 4,000lb to enable payloads of up

to 22,600lb to be carried. The wing pinion fuel tanks were retained. The cruising speeds were expected to be between 520 and 545mph at 23,500ft depending upon ambient temperature. Because of reduced block times, the Comet 4A would be able to operate economically on stages of around 500 miles. The high-speed cruise procedure showed advantages up to around 2,000 miles, but for distances in excess of this, the long-range cruise technique more applicable to the Comet 4 was used. The increase in speed helped to compensate for the higher fuel consumption, due to the reduced cruising height. Both the rate of climb and descent were increased, giving reduced block time due to the maximum possible distance for high-speed level cruise. In effect, although more fuel was burnt per hour of flight, this was largely compensated for by the shorter time in the air.

The airfield performance of the Comet 4A allowed unrestricted operations from the majority of international airports. At a take-off weight of 152,500lb a runway length of 6,500ft was required at sea level. The four-wheel bogie main under carriage gave a low ground pressure suitable for most runway surfaces.

At a launch sale for this new variant, Capital Airlines of the USA announced on 26 July 1956 a £19 million order for 14 Comet airliners. With deliveries commencing in late 1958, Capital were to have four Comet 4s, followed in the second half of 1959 by the Comet 4As.

Capital Airlines had pioneered the introduction of propeller turbine aircraft on US domestic services when the Viscount entered service in 1955. In the same year the airline carried 2.5 million fare-paying passengers flying over 31 million miles on a busy domestic network, with its base in Washington DC, linking the major cities of the eastern USA. The Comet 4As were to seat 74 passengers, 68

Below:
The Comet 3 returned to Heathrow Airport from the round-the-world flight on 28 December 1955.

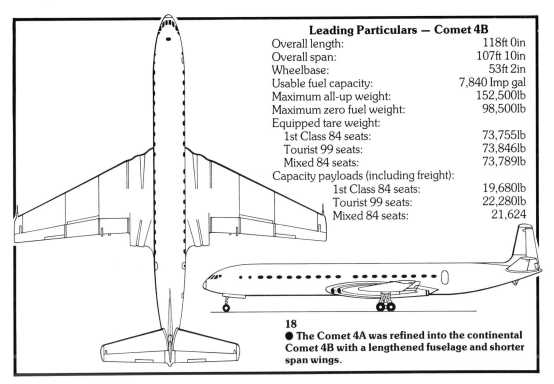

Leading Particulars — Comet 4B	
Overall length:	118ft 0in
Overall span:	107ft 10in
Wheelbase:	53ft 2in
Usable fuel capacity:	7,840 Imp gal
Maximum all-up weight:	152,500lb
Maximum zero fuel weight:	98,500lb
Equipped tare weight:	
1st Class 84 seats:	73,755lb
Tourist 99 seats:	73,846lb
Mixed 84 seats:	73,789lb
Capacity payloads (including freight):	
1st Class 84 seats:	19,680lb
Tourist 99 seats:	22,280lb
Mixed 84 seats:	21,624

18
● The Comet 4A was refined into the continental Comet 4B with a lengthened fuselage and shorter span wings.

four-abreast in two main cabins and the remaining six in a forward lounge. Unfortunately Capital Airlines experienced financial difficulties, eventually causing the airline to go into liquidation and the Comets were never delivered.

During the latter part of 1956, the Comet 3 prototype, G-ANLO in addition to conversion to Avon RA29 power, was adapted to take inter-changeable extension wingtips to allow aerodynamic development of both the Comet 4 and projected Comet 4A. G-ANLO emerged for engine runs of Avon RA29s on 13 February 1957 and rejoined the flight test programme on 25 February in a form closely representative of the Comet 4. In addition to the new engines in extensively modified bays with new larger intakes, modifications included elevator feel, airline standard flightdeck with the latest instrumentation and radio, full airframe de-icing and a developed air conditioning system.

In mid-1957, de Havilland released initial details of the continental Comet 4B which offered jet speed and comfort for the same cost as contemporary propeller turbine airliners. The increased seating

Below:
Following the Comet 4B, the ultimate Comet 4C was announced by de Havilland at the end of 1957, with the longer fuselage of the Comet 4B, and the long-range wings of the Comet 4. *Author*

capacity of up to 99 passengers gave a 15% reduction in seat-mile costs over route stages between 300 and 2,000 miles. With a 10% increase in seating capacity in a 118ft long fuselage the Comet 4B, extended by 38in, in effect replaced the 4A project. The wingspan of 107ft 10in was similar to the Comet 4A, but the pinion tanks were deleted. The maximum zero-fuel weight was increased by 2,500lb to 98,500lb. The all-up weight remained at 152,500lb, maintaining the flying characteristics, although the landing speed was slightly reduced due to the removal of the pinion tanks. The new aircraft retained the operational flexibility of the Comet 4A, allowing it to cruise at speeds between 520 and 545mph at 23,000ft. With this perfor-

mance the Comet 4B could carry a capacity payload of 20,000lb, representing 84 first class passengers and freight, over stages of up to 2,000 miles. By climbing to 38,000ft and cruising between 490 and 500mph, the same payload could be carried 2,600 miles.

British European Airways (BEA), now a part of British Airways, placed an initial order for six of the new Comet 4Bs to compete with the Air France-operated Caravelles on short-range jet operations in Europe. The 100-seat aircraft was to be operated on BEA's longer Mediterranean routes from 1960 to take the greatest advantage of the Comet's speed.

During its development programme, the

Top left:
The first production Comet 4, G-APDA, made its maiden flight from Hatfield on 27 April 1958.

Top right:
The first export order for the Comet 4 was for six aircraft for Aerolineas Argentinas, announced on 19 March 1958.

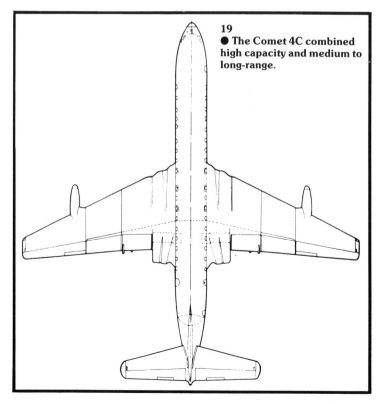

19
● The Comet 4C combined high capacity and medium to long-range.

Comet 3, G-ANLO, broke a number of city-to-city speed records. In fact, twice within eight days the aircraft, flown by John Cunningham, set up new records. On 16 October 1957, the Comet 3 flew nonstop from London to Khartoum, a distance of 3,064.1 miles in a time of 5hr 51min 14.8sec. This gave an average speed of 523.4mph. On the night of 23-24 October the 5,634.6 miles from London to Johannesburg was covered in 12hr 58min 57sec, including 53min on the ground at Khartoum. This represented an average speed of 490mph. Both flights were part of the programme of tropical and high altitude trials using the power of the Rolls-Royce Avon RA29 engines.

At the end of 1957, the ultimate Comet 4C development was announced, combining the high-density long fuselage of the Comet 4B with the long-range large-span wing of the Comet 4. This provided a substantially greater payload than the Comet 4, with a modest reduction in range. This aircraft in effect became the major export version of the Comet.

The Comet 4C thus combined the superior operating economics of the continental aircraft, with a payload-range capability only slightly less than the intercontinental Comet 4. This resulted in an economical aircraft with an operational versatility on a whole range of medium stages.

The intermediate Comet 4C was able to carry a payload of 21,785lb, such as 85 passengers in a mixed-class layout on stages up to a maximum of 2,475 miles, powered by the RA29 Avon engines identical to the other versions. Comet 4C was able to operate at Mach 0.74 at altitudes of 33,000ft. The maximum all-up weight was 156,000lb and landing weight was 118,500lb. At the maximum all-up weight take-off runway length was 6,770ft at 15°C at sea level.

As well as operating on the medium range Comet 4 routes with a greater payload capacity and slightly reduced range, the Comet 4C was able to operate on the shorter inter-city stages without any penalty in operating economics.

By the spring of 1958, Comet 4 production was well established at Hatfield and Chester. In early

February, the first Comet 4, G-APDA, for BOAC had its engines installed and had started resonance testing in the Hatfield experimental hangar. Other vital preparations continued including engine running, in preparation for the maiden flight which was made from Hatfield on 27 April 1958, commanded by John Cunningham.

The first export sale for the new Comet was announced on 19 March 1958, when Aerolineas Argentinas placed an order for six Comet 4s in a contract worth in excess of £9 million. The first of these aircraft was to enter service in 1959, with deliveries complete by 1960. The main centre of operations was Buenos Aires, halving existing flight times to New York and London.

Meanwhile the two Comet 2Es had been continuing the endurance flying on the new Rolls-Royce RA29 Avon engine, one of the aircraft on low-speed cruise, making a nonstop flight of 3,500 miles in a time of 8hr 6min, the longest Comet flight to date. The aircraft was operating out of London, touring around western and southern Europe, landed with 900gal of fuel, sufficient for a further hour of flying. As a result of the series of trials the engines were awarded the ARB approval and their overhaul life had reached 750hr with an imminent extension to 1,000hr.

Of the two aircraft allocated to the engine certification and endurance programme, G-AMXK was owned by BOAC and G-AMXD by the Ministry of Supply. Each aircraft had two 10,500lb thrust Avon RA29s fitted in the outer engine bays, with two standard 7,300lb thrust RA9 Avons inboard.

The first phase of the programme ending on 31 May 1958 called for 3,500 aircraft hours, equal to 7,000 engine hours, having started on 16 September 1957. Much of this flying was achieved by daily delights from London to Beirut and return, while other operations were to Nairobi and Gander. Because the RA29s were overpowering the aircraft, the RA9s were throttled back, to allow the more powerful engines to operate at their normal power.

The Comet 2 prototype, G-ALYT, was also fitted with one Rolls-Royce RA29 Avon in the starboard outer engine bay for icing tests of the engine and

Left:
One of the last duties for the Comet 2 prototype, G-ALYT, was icing trials for the RA29 Avon engine for the Comet 4.

Right:
The first Comet 4, G-APDA, was used for route-proving flights during the late summer of 1958.

Below right:
On 30 September 1958, BOAC's first two Comet 4s, G-APDB and G-APDC, were handed over at its engineering base at Heathrow, ready for operations to commence.
BOAC

intake, using a water rig fixed on the outside of the fuselage, in front of the intake. The most severe icing conditions were obtained by pumping distilled water from a pair of cabin-mounted 96gal Vampire fuel tanks into the spray rig at temperatures down to minus 30°C. The rig itself had to be heated with hot air to avoid premature freezing of the water. Observations could be made through a periscope and photographic recording was made on infrared film, which could better penetrate the spray, to determine the most effective method of ice removal. The aircraft retained the original cabin with square windows, and was therefore flown unpressurised.

On 28 March 1958, the BEA order for six Comet 4Bs was confirmed with the signature of the formal contract worth some £7 million. The cabin of the aircraft could be adapted to carry 87 mixed-class passengers (22 first class and 65 tourist) while an all-tourist layout could carry 102 passengers.

During the final preparations for service entry, by which time the Avon engines had been approved for 1,000 flying hours between overhaul, the Comet 4 was involved in a number of overseas proving flights.

On 12 September 1958, G-APDA helped celebrate the opening of the new 7,730ft-long runway at Hong Kong, Kai Tak airport. On the return it flew Hong Kong to London, 7,925 miles in three stages,

taking a total of 18hr 22min. The refuelling stops at Bombay and Cairo gave a total flying time of 16hr 16min, resulting in the fastest long-range flight in airliner history, up to that time.

The Comet had already been flown into New York Idlewild — now Kennedy Airport — by John Cunningham on 11 August to test its suitability for compliance with the engine noise regulations. On the return to Hatfield, an unofficial record time of 6hr 16min was achieved.

From 16-22 September, G-APDA made a tour of Canada and South America, visiting the major Canadian cities of Ottawa, Toronto, Montreal and Vancouver. It then flew via Mexico to Lima, Buenos Aires, Rio de Janeiro, Caracas and back via New York. During the 23,000-mile tour, VIP passengers were carried on various demonstrations. Probably one of the most demanding operations on the tour was the take-off from Mexico City with a full commercial load to Lima. The airfield elevation is 7,340ft, the temperature was about 25°C and the main runway was closed, requiring the use of the 8,200ft secondary runway.

On 30 September, the first two Comet 4s were handed over to BOAC at Heathrow Airport in a formal ceremony, and they were joined by a third aircraft on 3 October, poised for commercial jet operations to restart after the tragic demise of the Comet 1.

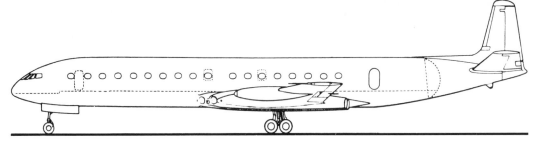

Comet 4 Into Service

Although the Comet 4 was intended for the BOAC Empire routes through Africa and to Asia, a spectacular start was made to the commercial services by inaugurating the world's first jet transatlantic service from London to New York. A pre-inaugural press flight was flown on 2 October 1958, followed by the start of regular jet operations on 4 October. The aircraft used on this historic occasion was Comet 4, G-APDC. By 14 November, the London to New York service was operating daily, having commenced initially as a weekly service.

In the late summer of 1958, East African Airways placed an order for two Comet 4s, later increased to three, to the same specification as BOAC for delivery by 1960. The Comets were to be used on the Nairobi to London service and also between

Nairobi and Bombay. More details also were released of the planned Aerolineas Argentinas operations with services commencing in May 1959 serving New York, Rio de Janeiro, Trinidad, Santiago, Dakar, Madrid, London, Paris, Frankfurt and Rome from Buenos Aires. The Aerolineas Comets were to be configured with 67-seat mixed-class interiors.

From 1 April 1959, BOAC introduced the Comet 4 on the Europe to Asia services, routes ideally suited to the aircraft. Gaining from the

Below:
The first North Atlantic jet airliner service was operated by BOAC between London and New York with Comet 4s, commencing on 4 October 1958.
BOAC

Above:
The East African Airways Comet 4s were to the same specification as BOAC.

Right:
BOAC did all its own Comet maintenance at its engineering base at Heathrow. *BOAC*

Below:
As more Comet 4s were delivered, BOAC introduced them to its south and eastbound routes, including as far as Cape Town in South Africa. *BOAC*

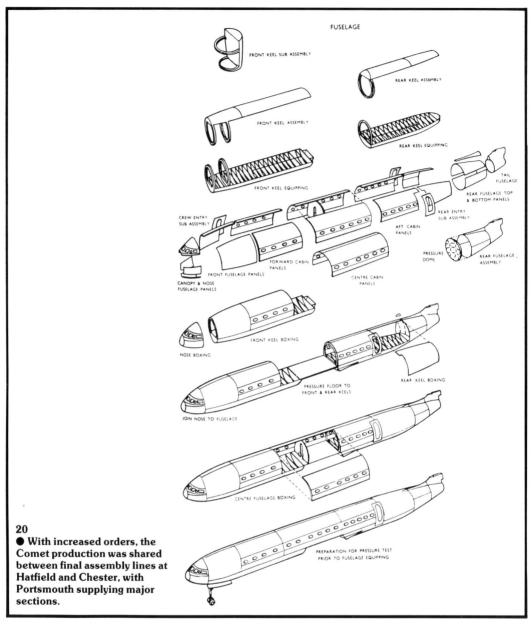

FUSELAGE

FRONT KEEL SUB ASSEMBLY

REAR KEEL ASSEMBLY

FRONT KEEL ASSEMBLY

REAR KEEL EQUIPPING

FRONT KEEL EQUIPPING

TAIL FUSELAGE

REAR FUSELAGE TOP & BOTTOM PANELS

CREW ENTRY SUB ASSEMBLY

REAR ENTRY SUB ASSEMBLY

AFT CABIN PANELS

PRESSURE DOME

REAR FUSELAGE ASSEMBLY

FORWARD CABIN PANELS

FRONT FUSELAGE PANELS

CANOPY & NOSE FUSELAGE PANELS

CENTRE CABIN PANELS

FRONT KEEL BOXING

NOSE BOXING

REAR KEEL BOXING

PRESSURE FLOOR TO FRONT & REAR KEELS

JOIN NOSE TO FUSELAGE

CENTRE FUSELAGE BOXING

PREPARATION FOR PRESSURE TEST PRIOR TO FUSELAGE EQUIPPING

20
● **With increased orders, the Comet production was shared between final assembly lines at Hatfield and Chester, with Portsmouth supplying major sections.**

30,000 flying hours on commercial service of the Comet 1, the Comet 4 was carrying twice the passengers on stages twice as long as the Comet 1, suiting it ideally for African, Asian and South American operations. The high power-to-weight ratio of the Comet 4 gave it a dramatic take-off and climb away from the hot and windless runways in the tropics. The long route to Tokyo was flown through a full range of climatic extremes with regularity and at a profit. The capability of the aircraft to operate commercially from existing airfields with little, if any, restrictions helped maintain regular schedules. Where the Comet 1 flew from London to Tokyo in over 36hr with eight stops, the Comet 4 carried greater payload with four stops in less than 26hr. The Comet was the right jet at the right time, ready to revolutionise travel standards and financial returns. This time, however, the competition was much closer, having had a chance to catch up and learn by de Havilland's misfortunes.

In the spring of 1959, the Comet 4 structural test specimen passed the 100,000hr mark in the water tank. Testing of the full specimen had commenced at the end of June 1958, and the milestone equivalent to 33 years of airline operations was passed at the beginning of March.

Aerolineas Argentinas became the first overseas operator of the Comet 4 when its first aircraft, LV-PLM, was delivered from Hatfield to Buenos Aires in the record time of 18½hr over 7,000 miles. The second Comet, LV-PLO, followed on 18 March, allowing the first jet operations in Latin America.

The first Comet 4B for BEA, G-APMA, was rolled off the Hatfield assembly line on 15 June 1959

BEA introduced the first of its Comet 4Bs into service on 1 April 1960.

Left:
Comet 4B, G-APMA, was the first for BEA and the first of this continental version of the Comet.

Below:
Olympic Airways announced its initial order in July 1959 for two Comet 4Bs to be operated in close co-operation with BEA.

Bottom:
Mexicana was the first customer for the high-density intercontinental Comet 4C.

Above right:
Misrair, later to become United Arab Airlines, operated a fleet of Comet 4Cs from its Cairo base.

Right:
MEA placed an order for four Comet 4Cs in January 1960 for operations from Beirut throughout Europe and Asia.

ready for its first flight on 27 June. While initial Comet 4 production was at Hatfield, this work was later transferred to Chester, and Hatfield concentrated on the Comet 4Bs. The Comet 4C was shared between the two factories.

On 20 July 1959, Olympic Airways, the Greek National Airline, announced its intention to acquire a pair of Comet 4Bs to be operated in co-operation with BEA. The operations centred in Athens were to serve European destinations as far as London and Amsterdam, and Middle Eastern centres such as Beirut and Cairo, starting in early 1960. BEA increased its order by one Comet 4B on 12 August, and the first aircraft, G-APMA, had flown about 100hr on its certification trials by 13 August; the certification flying included typical route-proving flights.

Meanwhile after three months of operation with Aerolineas Argentinas, the Comets had generated a 36% increase in traffic between South America and Europe, and a massive 84% increase on the South to North American routes. Load factors averaged out respectfully at 69.24% and 85.66%. The early success of jet operations was due to early delivery, good serviceability, high utilisation, ease of training of the crews and the high passenger appeal.

On 30 October 1959, Mexicana (CMA) signed for three Comet 4Cs, the first customer for the type, the first aircraft making its maiden flight from Hatfield the next day. The order had been anticipated in advance, but delays were also avoided by converting a BEA Comet 4B which had its extension wings changed, and relocating the

Comet 4B later down the production line. Based in Mexico City the Comets operated to Los Angeles, Chicago, and Havana, but due to financial problems with the airline, the aircraft were not widely used. To operate with the airline, American FAA airworthiness approval was obtained.

After its first year in service with BOAC, the Comet 4 had achieved a 40% increase in the airline's passenger traffic on all services across the North Atlantic. Earnings across the North Atlantic increased by 32% over the previous year. In the first 12 months, the Comet 4s carried 76,000 passengers, flew 6,377,000 miles over a total 15,150 revenue flying hours. The Comet's punctuality was better than any other BOAC aircraft, and reliability had been high with no engine failures in flight. The routes to Tokyo were also a success with passenger business increasing by 22%.

In addition to New York and Tokyo, Comet 4s were flying to Montreal, Santiago, Johannesburg and Melbourne, with many stops in between for passenger benefit. On the eastern routes, the Comet was achieving a high average utilisation of an 80% passenger load factor, a considerable improvement over other carriers. On the transatlantic route load factors in the high 80s and lower 90s were the norm.

The services across the South Atlantic commenced on 25 January 1960, the twice-weekly operation ending at Santiago, 7,950 miles from London, flown in an elapsed time of around 26hr. On 2 December 1959, Comets were back on the London to Johannesburg route, flying the 5,650 miles in about 17½hr. On 30 January 1960, the London to New York route was extended to the Caribbean, flying as far as Montego Bay in Jamaica, with intermediate stops at Nassau. Qantas chartered a BOAC Comet 4 for the Singapore to Sydney section of the joint Kangaroo service between Britain and Australia. As these routes developed through 1960, BOAC Comet 4s were flying well over 100,000 unduplicated route miles.

Early in 1960, Misrair — the national airline of Egypt, later to become United Arab Airlines and Egyptair — placed an initial order for three Comet 4Cs, worth about £4 million. The airline eventually ordered eight Comet 4Cs, its last one being the ultimate Comet built when it was delivered on 26 February 1964. The first aircraft was built at Chester and delivered to the airline in June 1960, only six months from order, covering such varied routes as the 2,200 miles from London to Cairo in under 5hr, and the much shorter Cairo to Beirut, replacing Viscounts.

BEA took delivery of the first two, G-APMB and G-APMC, of what was to become a fleet of 14

Comet 4Bs, at Hatfield on 16 November 1959. In addition, Olympic Airways operated four aircraft in close co-operation with BEA, where in effect their fleets were combined. By the time the summer schedules started with BEA on 1 April 1960, five Comets were in service with the airline. The

Below:
Olympic Comet 4B operations commenced on 18 May 1960, its fleet of four aircraft having two registered in Greece, and two in Britain. *Author*

Bottom:
The MEA Comet 4Cs entered service in January 1961 from a prosperous and peaceful Beirut, unlike today's chaos. *MEA*

Right:
Sudanair ordered two Comet 4Cs, the second aircraft being the last Hatfield-built Comet.

Below right:
The last new airline customer for the Comet 4C was Kuwait Airways, which ordered two prior to its order for Trident 1Es.

expanding Comet operations paved the way for the later and faster Trident with its automatic landing capability.

The delivery of Comet 4, G-APDJ, to BOAC on 11 January 1960, completed the total of 19 aircraft for the airline, only 16 months from the initial delivery and all ahead of schedule. In addition, three Comet 4s had been delivered to Aerolineas Argentinas, three Comet 4Bs to BEA and the first Comet 4C, XA-NAS for Mexicana, was delivered on 14 January. By this time, production was fully established at the Hatfield and Chester factories.

In January 1960, Middle East Airlines placed an order worth £5.5 million for four Comet 4Cs with an option on the fifth, which was not taken up. Operations were planned to commence in April 1961 from the Beirut base to London, Frankfurt, Athens and Bombay, as well as many other European and Middle Eastern destinations.

The first of the Olympic Comet 4Bs, SX-DAK, was delivered to Athens on 30 April 1960, followed by the second aircraft on 14 May, allowing services to commence on 18 May. The Olympic Comets were able to join the BEA fleet, following a number of ad hoc flights. Three routes were inaugurated on the start date: London-Rome-Athens-Istanbul, London-Rome-Athens-Tel Aviv and London-Moscow. In addition a London-Nice-London service was operated at short notice.

On 10 June 1960 the first Misrair Comet 4C, SU-ALC, was delivered to Cairo only 23 weeks after the order was placed. The second Comet,

SU-ALD, was delivered on 28 June and services commenced on 16 July, with a service from Cairo to London via Rome and Frankfurt.

East African Airways was the final airline to put the Comet 4 into service and which commenced scheduled operations on 17 September 1960 from Heathrow Airport to Nairobi.

The first MEA Comet 4C was accepted at Hatfield on 15 December 1960, the early delivery allowing scheduled services to commence on 5 January 1961, four months earlier than planned. Prior to this delivery MEA had chartered a Comet 4 from BOAC to build up operational experience.

The fifth Comet 4C was built against the option for MEA but, as this order was not confirmed, the aircraft was demonstrated at Farnborough in 1961 in MEA colours as G-AROV. It was then sold to Aerolineas Argentinas to replace one of its aircraft lost in an accident.

The last two airline customers for the Comet 4C were Sudan Airways which ordered two aircraft previously allocated to Mexicana, and two more were ordered by Kuwait Airways in preparation for the entry into service of its later Trident 1Es. The two Sudanair Comet 4Cs were delivered in December 1962, the second aircraft, ST-AAX, being the last Hatfield-built Comet. The first Kuwait Airways aircraft was delivered in January 1963, followed by the second one a year later.

A unique VIP Comet 4C, SA-R-7, was ordered by Saudi Arabian Airlines for the use of King Ibn Saud of Saudi Arabia. The aircraft was built at Hatfield with many special features, including a VIP front cabin and tourist seats in the rear cabin. First flight was on 29 March 1962, with the first overseas European flight in June. In August, the aircraft

Below:
A unique VIP Comet 4C was SA-R-7 for King Ibn Saud of Saudi Arabia, which crashed in the Alps on 20 March 1963. *Author*

Bottom:
BOAC flew its last Comet commercial flight with G-APDM arriving at Heathrow from New Zealand on 24 November 1965. *Author*

made its first visit to Jeddah, before crew training commenced at Hatfield in late September through most of October. Crew training continued with route-proving around Europe with occasional visits to Saudi Arabia. On 19 March 1963, the aircraft was requested to fly from Hatfield to Geneva and then commence a shuttle from Nice to Geneva, with King Saud and his retinue on board the first portion of the flight programme. On a later flight, the American Saudi Arabian Airlines crew were close to being cleared on the aircraft, so the de Havilland test pilot, John Hanslip, and flight engineer, Ken Rouse, were on board to monitor the operation. In

the early hours of 20 March 1963, with the de Havilland aircrew resting in a cabin after a long duty period, the aircraft struck the top of an Alpine ridge near Cuneo and all on board were killed.

BOAC withdrew its Comet 4s toward the end of 1965, the last commercial flight being with G-APDM from New Zealand to London on 24 November. Five of the early aircraft were acquired by Malaysian Airways, while the majority of the remainder were acquired by Dan-Air.

BEA and Olympic started to withdraw their Comet 4Bs in the spring of 1969, many of them being stored at Cambridge. The last Comet 4B service by BEA was from Malaga to Heathrow Airport on 31 October 1971 by G-APMA which was then withdrawn from use and scrapped at Heathrow the following year. A number of the Comet 4Bs were allocated to BEA Airtours at Gatwick which continued operations with the aircraft until early 1973, the last flight being with G-APMF on 31 January. Five of the aircraft stored at Cambridge were acquired by Channel Airways, which made very little alteration to either the BEA

Below:
Five of the early BOAC Comet 4s were sold to Malaysian Airways, later to become Malaysia-Singapore Airline (MSA). *Author*

Bottom:
Most of the remainder of the BOAC fleet were acquired by Dan-Air, which eventually became a major operator of a large fleet of Comet 4s of all versions. *Author*

or Olympic livery apart from changing the titles. Channel, however, went bankrupt on 1 February 1972 and its Comet 4Bs, together with the ones from BEA Airtours, were acquired by Dan-Air, some for service and others to be broken up for spares at Lasham.

Three of the four MEA Comet 4Cs were destroyed by the Israeli attack on Beirut Airport on 28 December 1968, and the surviving aircraft, OD-ADT, was sold to Dan-Air at the end of 1973 for spares.

Dan-Air progressively acquired the retired fleets of Malaysian, East African Airways, Egyptair, Sudanair and the one surviving Kuwait Airways aircraft. The Comet 4s were reduced to scrap for spares recovery while the remainder were put into service making Dan-Air the largest Comet fleet operator.

The final Comets in passenger service were the five ex-RAF Transport Command Comet C4s retired from service use at the end of July 1975. These five Comets were converted to civil operations by Dan-Air at its Lasham base and continued in service for another five years until the last commemorative Comet passenger flight was made by Dan-Air on 9 November 1980, in G-BDIW, which was later flown to Düsseldorf for preservation.

Top:
Following the retirement of Comet 4Bs by BEA in October 1971, when the Tridents were fully established, some were acquired by BEA Airtours at Gatwick until it retired them in January 1973. *Author*

Above:
Five of the ex-BEA and Olympic Comet 4Bs were acquired by the Southend-based Channel Airways, with very little change to the livery. *Author*

Top right:
Dan-Air acquired all the ex-Channel and BEA Airtours Comet 4Bs. *Author*

Above right:
The Egyptair Comet 4Cs were acquired by Dan-Air at Lasham for spares. *Author*

Right:
The penultimate Comet 4C, originally delivered to Kuwait Airways, was acquired by Dan-Air as G-AYVS, and finally broken up at Lasham in March 1978. *Author*

Bottom right:
Dan-Air acquired the five ex-RAF Comet C4s in excellent condition with many of the aircrew, finally retiring the Comets on 9 November 1980. *Author*

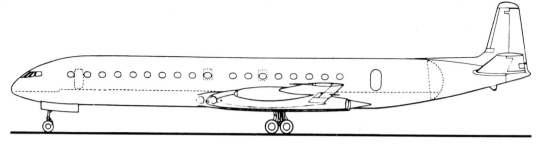

The RAF Comets

Following the completion of the Comet investigation and the publication of the findings, there were a number of Comet 2s, either completed for BOAC or in an advanced stage of construction. Three of the earliest aircraft remained with unmodified cabins and, under the cloak of much security, were extensively modified for signals duties. These aircraft had varied bathtub-shaped radomes fitted under the fuselage and were operated by No 192 Squadron from RAF Watton and later No 51 Squadron at Wyton on intelligence-gathering missions on the fringe of the Iron Curtain countries, until outdated by satellites. One of these aircraft was destroyed in a hangar fire at Wyton and replaced by a standard Comet C2 which was partially modified by Marshall of Cambridge before completing the equipment installation at Wyton.

In February 1955, the RAF placed an order for 10 Comet 2s, the first two initially to a TMk 2 training standard, and the remainder to a full passenger-carrying CMk 2. The two earlier aircraft were later modified to CMk 2 standard and all aircraft featured strengthened pressurised cabins with oval windows, amongst a number of other modifications to bring them in effect up to a full civil Certificate of Airworthiness standard for high-speed worldwide passenger operations.

The first Comet 2 for the RAF made its maiden flight on 9 December 1955. Meanwhile, No 216 Squadron had returned to RAF Lyneham on 10 November to disband after 38 years of unbroken service. Preparations then commenced to reform the squadron during 1956 as the RAF's first jet transport squadron.

On 7-8 June, the first two Comets were delivered to No 216 Squadron at Lyneham, the first official operation being a ministerial flight to Moscow for the Tushino Air Display on 24 June. By the middle of January 1957, a total of seven Comet 2s had

Below:
Specially adapted unpressurised Comet 2Rs were used by No 51 Squadron at Wyton for intelligence gathering. *Author*

been delivered to No 216 Squadron, accumulating a flying time of some 1,400hr on global operations as far away as the weapons test ranges at Woomera in Australia. Proving flights had commenced to Aden in September 1956 with Singapore as a destination in October. Malta and Cyprus were also regular destinations particularly during the Suez Crisis in October 1956.

The No 216 Squadron Comet 2s were able to offer high-speed jet transport worldwide at short notice. The aircraft supported V-bomber deployment, transport of troops and ships companies and VIP transport for government ministers. The VIPs also included the Queen and HRH Prince Philip on 4 June 1952, Her Majesty's first jet flight.

The squadron commenced full-scale jet transport operations with Comet 2s in early June 1957, by

which time all 10 aircraft had been delivered. All crew training and route-proving had been completed, and schedules were becoming established to Asia and Australia. In addition to the normal carriage of passengers the aircraft could be configured as an air ambulance capable of carrying stretcher and sitting patients.

As experience was built up, the Comet 2s, which had made a number of flights across the Atlantic to North America, were then extended to Christmas Island via San Francisco and Honolulu. Comets supported the V-bombers based at Pinecastle AFB in Florida for the USAF bombing competition. Regular Christmas Island operations commenced on 1 October 1957 in support of the nuclear test programme. The new service, covering 19,000 miles round trip, was operated weekly involving a flying time of 45¼hr over a period of three days and 18hr.

In the casualty evacuation role the RAF Comet 2s were ideal, bringing smooth, quiet and rapid transportation to injured or ill patients. It revolutionised the transportation of this often fragile human cargo, the flight time from Singapore for example being reduced from seven days to 19hr.

In general, up to 36 patients could be carried in one Comet 2, consisting of six stretchers in the forward cabin, eight reclining seats in the rear cabin and the remainder in the standard trooping seats with the medical team and other passengers. Normally, the patients were attended by two flight sisters and two male nursing staff, a medical officer being available at each stop if necessary. Normally, seriously ill patients were not carried, but if they were a medical officer could also accompany the flight. Normal seats could easily replace the stretchers for a positioning flight to allow the full complement of passengers to be carried. The RAF was responsible for the carriage by air of patients from all three Services, loading stretcher patients through the front crew entry door and up a special covered ramp, to protect the passenger from the elements.

In the first two years of operation, the first year being largely for training, No 216 Squadron flew 5.5 million miles in 12,000hr. The aircraft had operated on a worldwide basis in temperatures ranging from the Arctic cold of Labrador to the humid heat of Singapore. Distances varied from the short 200-mile hop from London to Paris, up to a 30,000-mile round-the-world flight. No major problems were encountered with ground or in-flight handling, including air traffic requirements.

Because of the demanding responsibilities of flying worldwide routes with all levels of passengers from Royalty to sick children, only the most experienced crews were chosen to operate the Comets. The reason was certainly not due to any special difficulties of operation. A captain would have a minimum of 1,500hr of command experience, of which 400hr would have been on four-engined aircraft. The average age of the aircrew members was 32-35 years old, with captains having 3,500hr flying time. Navigators, signallers and engineers had between 2,600 and 3,000hr experience. All captains and co-pilots were given a jet conversion course on Meteor jet trainers, followed by a short course at the Canberra OCU which was also for the navigators' benefit. The Comet conversion course consisted of 55hr by day and 20hr by night, broken down into 18hr dual training including an instrument rating; 17hr in command and 40hr supervised route flying.

On 5 September 1960, de Havilland announced that RAF Transport Command had selected five Comet 4C aircraft, to be known as the CMk 4, for delivery during 1961 and 1962. These new aircraft were to operate with No 216 Squadron alongside the existing CMk 2s to provide an additional longer range capacity. All the RAF Comet CMk 4s were built at Chester, the first one, XR395, making its maiden flight on 15 November 1961. Following a programme of crew training at Hatfield, all five aircraft were delivered to No 216 Squadron at Lyneham by 1 June 1962.

The Comet CMk 2s continued in service until March 1967, when XK698 made the last sortie before retirement of the aircraft from passenger operations. The Comet 2Rs with No 51 Squadron were finally withdrawn from service towards the end of 1974 when they were replaced by specially adapted Nimrods.

The Comet CMk 4s continued in operation with No 216 Squadron until the unit disbanded on 30 June 1975, a final commemorative flight being made by XR395 on 2 July from Lyneham over Heathrow and Hatfield to storage at Leconfield. All

Above left:
No 216 Squadron commenced full-scale jet operations with Comet 2s in mid-1957.

Above:
The Comet 2s were ideal for the casualty evacuation role.
Crown Copyright

Right:
Five of the longer-range Comet CMk 4s were ordered for No 216 Squadron in September 1960.

Below right:
The Comet C2s were retired from No 216 Squadron in March 1967, many being dispersed to ground training duties. XK716, the only Chester-built Comet 2, replaced G-ALYT at Halton.
Author

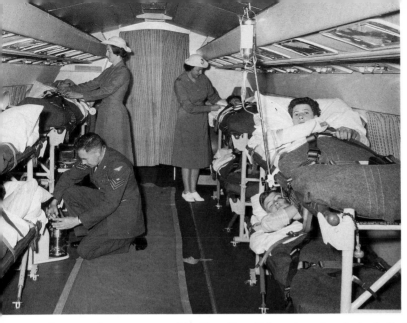

five aircraft were acquired by Dan-Air which took delivery of the fleet at Lasham on 3-4 September 1975.

When Comet production ceased there were still two airframes stored at the Chester factory. They were in fact Comet 4Cs, but when the Nimrod was ordered for maritime reconnaissance with the RAF as an adaptation of the Comet, these two aircraft were used in the development programme. Both aircraft had their fuselages shortened to the Comet 4 cabin length and the first, XV147, was flown from Chester to Woodford on 25 October 1965 for conversion to the Nimrod configuration. It flew as a Nimrod development aircraft on 31 July 1967, but retained throughout its life the RA29 Avon engines. The second aircraft, XV148, was converted at Chester, complete with Spey engines, and made its first flight on 23 May 1967 to

Woodford to join the flight development programme.

BOAC Comet 4, G-APDF, was acquired by the Ministry of Technology in February 1967, and was converted at Chester as XV814, where it acquired a bathtub-shaped radome under the forward fuselage and a balancing dorsal fin similar to the Nimrod. The aircraft was delivered to the Radio Department at Farnborough on 7 October 1968, where it is still in operation.

On delivery to Farnborough, this Comet had flown just over 22,000hr, and in the 21 years at the RAE, it has added a further 4,500hr. The reason for this relatively low utilisation is that by nature of its classified radio, radar and avionics trials, it spends long periods on the ground being fitted with specialist equipment. In its most recent trials programme, the aircraft has been further adapted for communications development, with the fin from Nimrod XV147. This fairing houses satellite/communications equipment, and its somewhat changed appearance has resulted in this venerable aircraft being known as the RAE Conrod.

Although it is now somewhat aged, the Comet still provides the RAE with a very useful vehicle for carrying a mass of specialised equipment to high altitudes and for long distances, anywhere in the world where trials need to be undertaken. There is also adequate room for crew, observers, and their kit and equipment.

As part of the abortive Nimrod AEW3 programme, ex-BOAC Comet 4, G-APDS, was acquired for the development of the Marconi radar on 30 January 1969, initially based at Boscombe Down. It was delivered to Woodford for the addition of the nose radome and officially rolled out on 1 March 1977. On completion of its part of the development programme, when the production standard conversions joined the flight testing, XW626 was delivered to the RAE Bedford, where it is currently stored in non-flying condition on the north side of the airfield. Another ex-BOAC Comet 4, G-APDP, was acquired by RAE Farnborough in 1973, but five years later it was derelict, probably used for spares for the aircraft still flying.

The only other Comet still operating could well be described as one careful owner, always kept under cover and only used occasionally, rather like an immaculate Morris Minor. This aircraft is Comet 4C, XS235, which first flew from Chester on 26 September 1963 to Hatfield. It was then fitted out with racks and interior fittings as a flying laboratory, before delivery to Boscombe Down on 2 December. At the time of writing, in its 26th year of operation, the total flying time had reached 7,500hr, and quite naturally the aircraft looks as good as new.

Low flying hours on the aircraft does not signify a low level of activity overall. Many of the experiments take time to install, calibrate and

ground test, before the ultimate airborne testing. For every hour of flight, between 10 and 20hr of data analysis is generated in the laboratory. The aircraft also has to be subjected to more than its fair share of non-destructive testing (NDT) of the structure, as it is in effect being treated as a fleet of one aircraft with no others able to share in the load.

This Comet, named *Canopus*, is operated by the Flying Division on behalf of the Radio and Navigation Division of Boscombe Down and is generally used for new avionics, mainly for navigation, plus radio altimeters and also for photographic work. The original underfuselage bathtub radome once used for Doppler trials has now been replaced by an aerial boat to carry communications aerials without penetrating the pressure hull.

The purpose of a flying laboratory is to give maximum space for the installation of equipment and carriage of flight observers. The aircraft needs to be equipped with a comprehensive range of radio and navigation aids of sufficiently high

accuracy and reliability to act as a standard for the equipment under test. Sufficient electrical power in whatever form required must be available to operate the systems and a high-capacity flexible data recording system is provided to record information from both the master reference systems and equipment under test, to carry out the post-flight analysis.

The Comet provides an ideal platform for the testing of systems under evaluation for transport and maritime aircraft. In the rear cabin are five dedicated trial stations, and adequate space for fitting additional equipment under test. The reference navigation system is centred round high

Below:
Comet 4, XV814, was later modified as a flying laboratory for the use of RAE Farnborough. *Author*

Right:
In its latest configuration Comet 4, XV814, has a fin fitted from Nimrod prototype XV148 to assist in satellite communications.

quality inertial systems, which continuously produce aircraft position, velocity, heading and altitude. This datum equipment includes an old but accurate Decca Mk 19 and a pair of Litton inertial navigation systems uniquely assembled for Boscombe Down with top-grade specially selected Z-gyros on all three axes.

All data is recorded on magnetic tape once per second using a Plessey GPS receiver and an STC five-channel GPS receiver. The reference area in the forward cabin contains three seats for the datum manager, an assistant and a controller of the recording systems. A print out is made every minute to ensure that the equipment is still functioning. The onboard recording system has sufficient capacity to log the required parameters from the datum equipment, and monitor the large amounts of data from the equipment under test for up to the maximum 6hr endurance of the Comet. A number of interface units have also been developed to enable a variety of data streams to be recorded.

Over a two-year period the Comet flew 150hr to evaluate seven different inertial navigation systems for the Nimrod MR2 update programme. It is not usually the accuracy of the systems which is in any doubt, but more checking the operational performance.

In the spring of 1989, all the ground-based radio antennae of the Radio Trials Facility at the A&AEE were recalibrated using the Comet with its fit of highly accurate antennae. The facility is constantly in use for all Controller Aircraft (CA) Release trials of communications and radio navigation equipment with the associated aerial installations.

During the summer of 1989, 56hr were flown in support of an international test programme, evaluating GPS Navstar user equipment. For this purpose, the Comet was based at Thule AFB in Northern Greenland, allowing flights over the North Pole and back in 4½hr. This was a NATO programme sponsored by the joint programme office at HQ Space Command in Los Angeles. Those flights were made over the geographic North Pole, which is where inertial systems can have the greatest problem due to attenuation on the ice cap. The Rockwell Collins GPS receivers were the main units under evaluation, but a bonus was also the chance to test British-built systems at the same time.

This Comet came to the British Aerospace Open Day at Hatfield on 1 July 1989, to celebrate the 40th anniversary of the first flight of the prototype Comet by John Cunningham. At the rate it is flying, and bearing in mind the excellent condition of the aircraft, there is probably no reason why it should not be around to celebrate the 50th anniversary as well. Its graceful lines and spritely performance are still good, even by today's standards of high technology.

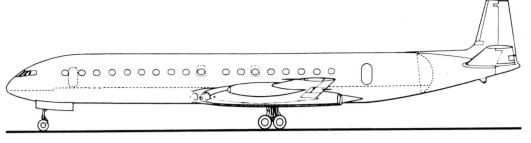

Appendices

Appendix I
Preserved Comets

C/N	Reg	Srs	Owner	Preserved
6013	G-ANAV	1A	BOAC	Nose in Science Museum, London
6020	F-BGNX	1A	AF	Fuselage to Mosquito Aircraft Museum 20/03/85
6022	G-APAS	1A	AF	Cosford Aerospace Museum in BOAC markings
6023	XK655	2R	RAF	Retired to Strathallan 21/08/74
6030	XK695	2R	RAF	Retired to Duxford 11/01/75
6035	XK699	C2	RAF	Lyneham, gate duty
6403	G-APDB	4	BOAC	Presented by Dan-Air 12/02/74 to Duxford Aviation Society
6407	XV814	4	RAE	Current flying condition
6419	XW626	4	RAE	Static storage at RAE Bedford, last flown 28/08/81
6420	G-APDT	4	BOAC	Escape training at London Heathrow
6422	G-APMB	4B	Dan-Air	Ground training at Gatwick
6424	XA-NAR	4C	CMA	Everett Community College, Washington, USA 01/85
6425	XA-NAS	4C	CMA	City of Chicago to Air and Space Museum, Washington 1989
6438	G-APYD	4B	Dan-Air	Science Museum, Wroughton 01/11/79
6470	G-BDIW	4C	Dan-Air	Retired to Düsseldorf 07/02/81, ex-XR398
6473	XS235	4C	A&AEE	Current flying condition

Abbreviations

C/N	Construction number
Reg	Registration
f/f	First flight
d/d	Date delivered
H	Hatfield
C	Chester
WFU	Withdrawn from use
BU	Broken up
WO	Written off
DBR	Damaged beyond repair

Appendix II
Comets manufactured by the de Havilland Aircraft Co at Hatfield, Herts, and Hawarden, Chester — Specifications and data

Data on all Mks	Srs 1	Srs 1A	Srs C2	Srs 3	Srs 4	Srs 4A	Srs 4B	Srs 4C
Span	115ft	115ft	115ft	114.8ft	114.8ft	107.8ft	107.8ft	114.8ft
Length	93.1ft	93.1ft	96.1ft	111.5ft	111.5ft	114.83ft	118ft	118ft
Height	28.5ft	28.5ft	28.5ft	28.5ft	28.5ft	28.5ft	28.5ft	28.5ft
Wing area	2,105sq ft	2,105sq ft	2,027sq ft	2,121sq ft	2,121sq ft	2,059sq ft	2,059sq ft	2,121sq ft
All-up weight (max)	105,000lb	115,000lb	120,000lb	145,000lb	160,000lb	152,500lb	158,000lb	162,000lb
Cruising speed	450mph	450mph	480mph	500mph	503mph	522mph	532mph	503mph
Cruising height	35,000ft	40,000ft	40,000ft	40,000ft	42,000ft	23,500ft	23,500ft	39,000ft
Max range with full payload (in miles)	1,500	1,770	2,535	2,700	3,225	2,730	2,500	2.650
No of passengers (max)	36	44	44	78	81	92	101	101
Engines (4)	Ghost 50 Mk 1	Ghost 50 Mk 1	Avon Mk 117	Avon 502	Avon 524	Avon 524	Avon 524	Avon 525B
Static thrust	4,450lb st	5,000lb st	7,300lb st	10,000lb st	10,500lb st	10,500lb st	10,500lb st	10,500lb st
Total tankage (imp gal)	6,000	6,906	6,906	8,360	8,900	7,800	7,800	8,900

Note: Comet 3B had span of 107.8ft and wing area of 2,059sq ft.

Appendix III
DH106 Comet Production

C/N	Reg	f/f	d/d	Owner	Built	Type	Remarks
6001	G-ALVG	27.07.49	—	MOS	H	P	Structural test at RAE 1954
6002	G-ALZK	27.07.50	02.04.51	MOS	H	P	BOAC route-proving, BU 3/57
6003	G-ALYP	09.01.51	08.04.52	BOAC	H	1	Lost off Elba 10/01/54
6004	G-ALYR	28.07.51	17.05.52	BOAC	H	1	Structural test at RAE 6/55
6005	G-ALYS	08.09.51	04.02.52	BOAC	H	1	BU at RAE 1955
6006	G-ALYT	16.02.52	—	MOS	H	2X	Prot Srs 2, to Halton 15/06/59
6007	G-ALYU	13.12.51	06.03.52	BOAC	H	1	RAE water tank testing 1954
6008	G-ALYV	09.04.52	23.04.52	BOAC	H	1	Lost near Calcutta 02/05/53
6009	G-ALYW	25.02.52	14.06.52	BOAC	H	1	RAE for structural testing, 1955
6010	G-ALYX	09.07.52	25.07.52	BOAC	H	1	Testing at Hatfield and RAE 1955
6011	G-ALYY	10.09.52	23.09.52	BOAC	H	1	Lost off Stromboli 08/04/54
6012	G-ALYZ	23.09.52	30.09.52	BOAC	H	1	Failed to take off, Rome 26/10/52
6013	G-ANAV	11.08.52	—	BOAC	H	1A	Ex-CPA CF-CUM, flight test at RAE 1954
6014	CF-CUN	24.12.52	02.03.53	CPA	H	1A	Destroyed at Karachi 02/03/53
6015	F-BGSA	13.11.52	11.12.52	UAT	H	1A	WFU 12/04/54 at Le Bourget
6016	F-BGSB	21.01.53	19.02.53	UAT	H	1A	WFU 12/04/54 at Le Bourget
6017	VC5301	21.02.53	18.03.53	RCAF	H	1A	412 Sqn, retired 3/10/64
6018	VC5302	25.03.53	13.04.53	RCAF	H	1A	412 Sqn, retired 3/10/63, CF-SVR
6019	F-BGSC	15.04.53	30.04.53	UAT	H	1A	DBR 25/06/53 Dakar
6020	F-BGNX	06.05.53	12.06.53	AF	H	1A	G-AOJT at RAE 1956 and dismantled
6021	F-BGNY	22.05.53	07.07.53	AF	H	1A	G-AOJU, XM829 at A&AEE
6022	F-BGNZ	16.03.53	22.07.53	AF	H	1A	G-APAS, XM823 DH Props, 27 MU 08/04/68

6023	G-AMXA	29.08.53	17.02.58	RAF	H	2R	XK655 51 Sqn, Strathallan 1974
6024	G-AMXB	03.11.53	08.06.56	RAF	H	T2	XK669 216 Sqn, burned Brize Norton 1968
6025	G-AMXC	25.11.53	12.07.57	RAF	H	2R	XK659 51 Sqn, retired 13/05/74
6026	G-AMXD	20.08.54	29.08.57	MOS	H	2E	RA29 trials, XN453, RAE Bedford
6027	XK663	18.07.55	19.04.57	RAF	H	2R	ex-G-AMXE, 51 Sqn, burned out 03/06/59
6028	XK670	12.03.56	07.06.56	RAF	H	T2	ex-G-AMXF, 216 Sqn, burned Lyneham 1968
6029	XK671	16.07.56	22.08.56	RAF	H	C2	ex-G-AMXG, 216 Sqn, Topcliffe 11/66
6030	XK695	21.08.56	14.09.56	RAF	H	C2	ex-G-AMXH, 216 Sqn, then 2R 51 Sqn
6031	XK696	29.09.56	14.11.56	RAF	H	C2	ex-G-AMXI, 216 Sqn, Watton 27/10/66
6032	XK697	17.11.56	12.12.56	RAF	H	C2	ex-G-AMXJ, 216 Sqn, 51 Sqn, Wyton
6033	G-AMXK	10.07.57	26.08.57	MOS	H	2E	RA29 trials, Smiths XV144 BLEU
6034	XK698	13.12.56	09.01.57	RAF	H	C2	216 Sqn, Shawbury, St Athan BU 1973
6035	XK699	02.02.57	20.02.57	RAF	H	C2	216 Sqn, Henlow 13/06/67, Lyneham
6036	—	—	—	MOS	H	2	Structural test specimen
6037	XK715	26.04.57	22.05.57	RAF	H	C2	216 Sqn, Cosford 1966, scrapped 5/73
6045	XK716	06.05.57	07.05.57	RAF	C	C2	216 Sqn, Halton, scrapped 1973
6100	G-ANLO	19.07.54	21.06.61	MOS	H	3	XP915 at BLEU Bedford as 3B
6101	—	—	—	MOS	H	3	Structural test specimen
6401	G-APDA	27.04.58	24.02.59	BOAC	H	4	Malaysian 9M-AOA, 9V-BAS, Dan-Air
6402	—	—	—	—	H	4	Structural test specimen
6403	G-APDB	27.07.58	30.09.58	BOAC	H	4	MSA 9M-AOB, Dan-Air, Duxford
6404	G-APDC	23.09.58	30.09.58	BOAC	H	4	MSA 9M-AOC, 9V-BAT, Dan-Air
6405	G-APDD	05.11.58	18.11.58	BOAC	H	4	MSA 9M-AOD, Dan-Air
6406	G-APDE	20.09.58	02.10.58	BOAC	C	4	MSA 9M-AOE, 9V-BAU, Dan-Air
6407	G-APDF	11.12.58	31.12.58	BOAC	H	4	RAE as XV814, current
6408	LV-PLM	27.01.59	02.03.59	AA	H	4	To LV-AHN, Dan-Air
6409	G-APDH	21.11.58	06.12.58	BOAC	C	4	WO Singapore 22/03/64 after fire
6410	LV-PLO	25.02.59	18.03.59	AA	H	4	To LV-AHO, WO 20/02/60 Buenos Aires
6411	LV-PLP	24.03.59	02.05.59	AA	H	4	To LV-AHP, WO 27/08/59 Asunción
6412	G-APDK	02.01.59	12.02.59	BOAC	C	4	Dan-Air, retired 07/05/73
6413	G-APDL	27.04.59	06.05.59	BOAC	H	4	Dan-Air, wheels-up landing 07/10/70
6414	G-APDM	21.03.59	16.04.59	BOAC	C	4	OD-AEV MEA, 9V-BBJ MSA, Dan-Air
6415	G-APDN	29.05.59	10.06.59	BOAC	H	4	Dan-Air, crashed 03/07/70 near Barcelona
6416	G-APDO	29.04.59	14.05.59	BOAC	C	4	Dan-Air, retired 02/07/73
6417	G-APDP	29.05.59	11.06.59	BOAC	C	4	MSA 9V-BBH, Dan-Air, RAE XX944
6418	G-APDR	09.07.59	20.07.59	BOAC	C	4	CMA as XA-NAP 03/12/64, Channel for spares
6419	G-APDS	06.08.59	14.08.59	BOAC	C	4	AEW Nimrod development as XW626
6420	G-APDT	02.10.59	19.10.59	BOAC	C	4	CMA as XA-NAB, BOAC ground trainer
6421	G-APMA	27.06.59	20.12.59	BEA	H	4B	WFU 25/01/72 at LHR and BU
6422	G-APMB	17.08.59	09.11.59	BEA	H	4B	Channel 6/70, Dan-Air, Gatwick
6423	G-APMC	01.10.59	16.11.59	BEA	H	4B	Airtours, Dan-Air 11/73, WFU 09/74
6424	XA-NAR	31.10.59	08.06.60	CMA	H	4C	Westernair N888WA 1973
6425	XA-NAS	03.12.59	14.01.60	CMA	H	4C	Westernair N999WA 1973
6426	G-APMF	05.01.60	27.01.60	BEA	H	4B	Airtours, Dan-Air 31/01/73, BU 10/75
6427	G-APDG	12.11.59	28.11.59	BOAC	C	4	Kuwait as 9K-ACI, Dan-Air, BU 06/74
6428	G-APDI	07.12.59	18.12.59	BOAC	C	4	To Ecuador as HC-ALT 1966, BU Miami
6429	G-APDJ	23.12.59	11.01.60	BOAC	C	4	Dan-Air 05/67, BU 06/74
6430	LV-POY	15.02.60	08.03.60	AA	H	4	LV-AHR crashed Sao Paulo 23/11/61
6431	VP-KPJ	14.07.60	25.07.60	EAA	C	4	5X-AAO, Dan-Air, BU 1972
6432	LV-POZ	18.02.60	19.03.60	AA	C	4	LV-AHS, Dan-Air as G-AZLW, BU 1973

6433	VP-KPK	28.07.60	06.09.60	EAA	C	4	5H-AAF, Dan-Air 1971, BU 1972
6434	LV-PPA	02.07.60	26.07.60	AA	C	4	LV-AHU, Dan-Air as G-AXIY, WFU 10/75
6435	G-APMD	17.03.60	29.03.60	BEA	H	4B	Airtours, Dan-Air 9/72, BU 1975
6436	G-APME	26.04.60	10.05.60	BEA	H	4B	Airtours, Dan-Air 1972, BU 10/78
6437	G-APYC	07.04.60	26.04.60	OLYM	H	4B	SX-DAK, BEA, Channel, Dan-Air, Kemble
6438	G-APYD	03.05.60	14.05.60	OLYM	H	4B	SX-DAL, Airtours, Channel, Dan-Air
6439	SU-ALC	21.05.60	10.06.60	UAA	C	4C	Crashed 02/01/71 near Tripoli
6440	G-APZM	30.06.60	14.07.60	OLYM	H	4B	SX-DAN, Channel, Dan-Air 1972
6441	SU-ALD	15.06.60	29.06.60	UAA	C	4C	Crashed 28/07/63 into sea near Bombay
6442	G-APMG	25.07.60	31.07.60	BEA	H	4B	Airtours 1970, Dan-Air 1973, BU 1978
6443	XA-NAT	07.10.60	29.11.60	CMA	H	4C	Damaged on landing Mexico City 01/12/70
6444	SU-ALE	22.11.60	23.12.60	UAA	C	4C	Crashed on take-off from Munich 09/02/70
6445	OD-ADK	03.12.60	19.12.60	MEA	H	4C	OD-ADR, WO Beirut 28/12/68
6446	OD-ADQ	04.02.61	15.02.61	MEA	C	4C	WO Beirut 28/12/68 by Israelis
6447	F-ARDI	18.03.61	25.03.61	OLYM	H	4B	SX-DAO, Airtours, Channel, BU 04/72
6448	OD-ADS	05.03.61	14.03.61	MEA	C	4C	WO Beirut 28/12/68 by Israelis
6449	G-ARCO	05.04.61	13.04.61	BEA	H	4B	Crashed in sea off Turkey 12/10/67
6450	OD-ADT	09.03.61	18.03.61	MEA	C	4C	Dan-Air for spares, BU 1974
6451	G-ARCP	11.04.61	19.04.61	BEA	H	4B	Airtours 1970, G-BBUV Dan-Air, BU 1978
6452	G-ARJK	04.05.61	15.05.61	BEA	C	4B	Airtours 1970, Dan-Air 1973, BU 1977
6453	G-ARGM	27.04.61	06.05.61	BEA	H	4B	Airtours 1970, Dan-Air 1973, BU 06/75
6454	SU-ALL	30.05.61	12.06.61	UAA	C	4C	Retired 02/06/75
6455	G-ARJL	19.05.61	31.05.61	BEA	H	4B	Olympic 1964, Airtours 1970, Dan-Air 11/73, BU 1974
6456	G-ARJM	08.06.61	26.06.61	BEA	C	4B	Crashed after take-off Ankara 21/12/61
6457	ST-AAW	05.11.62	14.11.62	Sudan	H	4C	Dan-Air 1975 as G-ASDZ, BU
6458	SU-ALM	30.06.61	15.07.61	UAA	C	4C	Retired 06/04/76, Dan-Air as G-BEEX 1976
6459	G-ARJN	21.07.61	04.08.61	BEA	H	4B	Airtours 1970, Dan-Air 1973, BU 1978
6460	G-AROV	21.08.61	27.04.62	AA	C	4C	LV-PTS, LV-AIB, Dan-Air 1971, BU 1978
6461	SA-R-7	29.03.62	15.06.62	Saudi	H	4C	Crashed in Alps 20/03/63
6462	SU-AMV	25.03.62	06.04.62	UAA	C	4C	Retired 31/05/76, Dan-Air as G-BEEY 1976
6463	ST-AAX	08.12.62	21.12.62	Sudan	H	4C	Dan-Air 07/75 as G-BDIF
6464	SU-AMW	03.04.62	16.04.62	UAA	C	4C	Crashed 19/07/62 in Thailand
6465	9K-ACA	14.12.62	18.01.63	Kuwait	C	4C	Dan-Air as G-AYWX 01/71, BU 1978
6466	SU-ANC	08.12.62	22.12.62	UAA	C	4C	Retired 16/12/75, Dan-Air as G-BEEZ 09/76
6467	XR395	15.11.61	01.06.62	RAF	C	C4	216 Sqn, retired 02/07/75, G-BDIT with Dan-Air. Then to Blackbushe, BU 8/84
6468	XR396	28.12.61	12.03.62	RAF	C	C4	216 Sqn, Dan-Air 09/75 as G-BDIM
6469	XR397	17.01.62	15.02.62	RAF	C	C4	216 Sqn, Dan-Air 09/75 as G-BDIV
6470	XR398	13.02.62	16.03.62	RAF	C	C4	216 Sqn, Dan-Air 09/75 as G-BDIW
6471	XR399	20.03.62	26.04.62	RAF	C	C4	216 Sqn, Dan-Air 09/75 as G-BDIX
6472	VP-KRL	12.03.62	10.04.62	EAA	C	4	5Y-AAA, Dan-Air 1971, BU 1972
6473	XS235	26.09.63	02.12.63	A&AEE	C	4C	Current 1989
6474	9K-ACE	17.12.63	02.02.64	Kuwait	C	4C	Dan-Air as G-AYVS 08/04/72, BU 1978
6475	SU-ANI	04.02.64	26.02.64	UAA	C	4C	Crashed Addis Ababa 14/01/70
6476	XV147	25.10.65	—	MoD	C		Nimrod prototype f/f 31/07/67, Avon engines
6477	XV148	23.05.67	—	MoD	C		Nimrod prototypes converted at Chester — Spey power

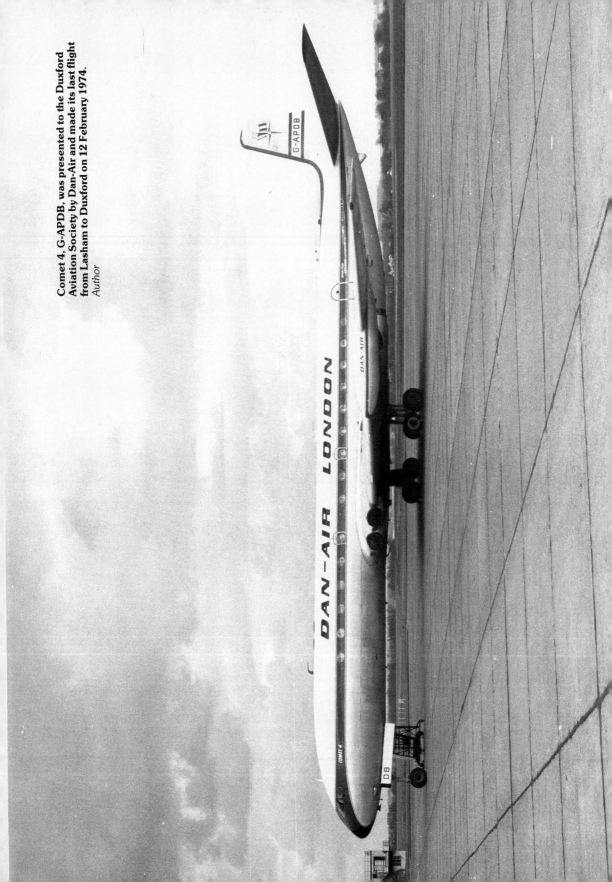

Comet 4, G-APDB, was presented to the Duxford Aviation Society by Dan-Air and made its last flight from Lasham to Duxford on 12 February 1974.
Author